WORK
WELL
BEING

*Leading thriving teams in
rapidly changing times*

MARK McCRINDLE
& ASHLEY FELL

ROCKPOOL

To Ruth, with whom this adventure of life is a great joy
and who, along with our children Acacia, Jasper, Zari,
Brighton and Corban, brings immeasurable flourishing.

MARK McCRINDLE

To my husband Michael and my mum Marja, my
greatest examples of hard work and authentic
leadership, and who encourage me to achieve more
than I ever thought possible.

ASHLEY FELL

A Rockpool book
PO Box 252
Summer Hill
NSW 2130
Australia

rockpoolpublishing.co
Follow us! **f ⊙** rockpoolpublishing
Tag your images with #rockpoolpublishing

ISBN: 978-1-925924-19-0

Published in 2020 by Rockpool Publishing
Copyright text © McCrindle Research 2020
Copyright images © McCrindle Research 2020

www.workwellbeing.com.au

Authors: Mark McCrindle and Ashley Fell
Data visualisation and illustrations: Ben Duffin
Cover device designer: Hendrik Zuidersma-Ros
Design by Sara Lindberg, Rockpool Publishing
Editing and index by Lisa Macken

A catalogue record for this
book is available from the
National Library of Australia

Printed and bound in China
10 9 8 7 6 5 4 3

CONTENTS

ABOUT THE AUTHORS

MARK MCCRINDLE

Award-winning social researcher Mark McCrindle (BSc Psychology, MA) has an international following and is recognised as a leader in tracking emerging issues and researching social trends. An engaging public speaker attributed with naming the next generation Generation Alpha, Mark regularly appears across many television networks and other media and is an influential thought leader, TEDx speaker and principal of McCrindle Research. This advisory, communications and research company counts among its clients more than 100 of Australia's largest companies and leading international brands.

Along with co-authoring Work Wellbeing, Mark is the author of three books on emerging trends and social change: The ABC of XYZ: Understanding the Global Generations, Word Up: A Lexicon and Guide to Communication in the 21st Century and The Power of Good. He and his wife Ruth have five children spanning the Generation Z and Generation Alpha age groups.

ASHLEY FELL

Ashley Fell is a social researcher, TEDx speaker and director of communications at internationally recognised company McCrindle Research. As a trends analyst and media commentator, she understands how to effectively communicate and inspire across diverse audiences. In addition to delivering keynote presentations at conferences, Ashley conducts training days for corporate and not-for-profit clients, facilitates panels across an array of industries and supervises workshops for diverse generations, covering generational change to technological disruption and key demographic transformations to social shifts.

Ashley and her husband Michael are based in Sydney, Australia and enjoy reading, travelling and spending time with Ashley's Gen Alpha nieces and nephews.

INTRODUCTION

When you picked up this book, was it the word *wellbeing* that sparked your interest? The use of the word in 21st-century vocabulary and discussion about the subject itself have increased in prevalence, but is it an applicable, useful term or just another buzzword? A Google search on the term tells us that wellbeing is the 'state of being comfortable, healthy or happy'. Today people place real focus on wellbeing, and it's not hard to figure out why.

The current century has ushered in some amazing advances in technology, and it's almost impossible to believe we've had smart phones for just a little over a decade. Prior to that mobile phones were indeed just that: phones – whereas today they are so much more: cameras, encyclopaedias, maps, games devices, music players, calculators, alarm clocks, wallets and so many other services we access daily.

The internet is another service that has transformed our work and personal lives. In our presentations we often say that some of the scariest things in the world are not physical threats but, rather, symbols. Instead of fearing snakes, spiders and heights, the bigger fears we hold are of symbols. We dread seeing the low WiFi symbol, indicating we can't connect to the world around us, and watching the buffering circle while waiting for something to load. But the scariest of them all would have to be the low battery symbol, when all forms of connectivity cease to exist.

These symbols we identify to our audience as being alarming are meant to be humorous and almost always yield a laugh. However, as with many jokes there is an element of truth behind it, and the fear of not being globally connected is a very real one. Technologies have also bought positive changes to our lives. The invention of the internet brought with it an incredible ability to connect globally with family and friends and engage with any piece of information at the click of a button (or, rather, the touch of a screen). Social media allows us to share every aspect of our lives with those we love, who may live thousands of kilometres away.

During the COVID-19 crisis, the spheres of business and education embraced Zoom and other digital meeting technologies to great effect. Most of us were grateful to have such connectivity in a period of isolation, yet it also became evident that virtual meetings had their limitations. Along with its inordinate benefits, technology has also brought with it some unique challenges, particularly to our wellbeing. It has blurred the lines of private and public; of school and home; of work and rest. It has made it harder for us to switch off, to connect with the physical world around us and to be present.

Even beyond the internet, online communities facilitated through social media platforms such as Instagram and Snapchat provide us with so much information about the lives of others that we now spend an inordinate amount of time comparing ourselves to everyone else's highlight reels. This is indicated in the popular acronym 'FOMO', or fear of missing out. While the internet and social media can facilitate increasingly connected communities, paradoxically they can also make us feel more isolated and fuel comparisons to others, negatively impacting our health and wellbeing. Interestingly, many a Baby Boomer and Gen Xer have confessed to us that when looking at the frantic activity on social media it is not FOMO (fear of missing out) they feel, but rather JOMO (joy of missing out)!

Currently, around one in four young people aged 15 to 19 meet the criteria for having a probable serious mental illness. Of concern, there has been a significant increase in the proportion of young people meeting this criteria; data shows that it increased by more than 20% in the most recent five-year period.[1] According to global research, mental illness contributes to 45% of the global burden of disease among those aged 10 to 24 years.[2]

Clearly the increased use of technology in our lives and the impact it has on our mental health and wellbeing, particularly that of younger people, is a significant challenge for our schools, families and communities.

The trend of wellbeing in schools has been steadily increasing over time. According to our future of education report,[3] in the last five years almost half of parents (48%) have increased their expectations of their child's school to support wellbeing. More than one in four (27%) have significantly or somewhat increased their expectations.

Generation Y parents are driving this expectation inflation with three in 10 (31%) significantly or somewhat increasing their expectations of schools compared to almost one in four Generation X parents (23%). Almost all parents (97%) believe schools should have a holistic focus and play some role in the management of wellbeing, with almost half (46%) believing schools should provide individualised support for wellbeing but refer on to other experts.

Compounding this challenge for young people's health and wellbeing is the mounting pressure that is put on them. According to parents, three in five (60%) believe the greatest challenge for students today is online bullying through social networks, followed by high pressure to do well in exams and assessments (51%) and the fact that life is more complicated, causing additional stress (49%).[4]

We recently interviewed Stephen Harris, the co-founder and director of learning at LearnLife Barcelona, the first in a worldwide network of learning hubs meant to accelerate change in existing education models through personal purpose-based learning.[5] Regarding student wellbeing, Stephen said:

There has been a significant backwards slide with mental health issues in the last five or six years. I think it's totally linked to an overemphasis on assessments and examinations by both the media and parents. I'm not condemning parents, because in many cases, they don't know enough about the system to understand what it's doing to the kids. Yet we keep selling the idea that the only pathway is to buckle down and study all these things. I would say in the last five years there has been a pronounced increase in the volume of kids who are suffering from anxiety. And then that also tips over into kids with severe anxiety, or severe depression.

Our schools and communities obviously have work to do when it comes to the mental health and wellbeing of student communities.

Mental health is far more than the absence of clinical conditions such as depression or anxiety. The World Health Organization defines mental health in a holistic context as 'a state of wellbeing in which every individual realises his or her own potential, can cope with the normal stresses of life, can work productively and fruitfully, and is able to make a contribution to her or his community'.[6]

Our comparison culture and the inability to switch off, combined with other life pressures and stresses, affect our mental health and wellbeing. Technology and the rise of the knowledge economy (where many more workers make their contributions by using digital tools rather than mechanised ones) mean we are sitting more and exercising less, and that we are working longer per week and later in life. Technology not only affects our mental health, it affects our physical health as well.

Although it is largely undisputed that eating well and getting regular exercise are key to overall health and wellbeing, over time there has been a shift away from viewing 'health' as being purely about the physical. Beyond health, the word 'wellbeing' also refers to more than just being physically and mentally healthy. The holistic approach to wellbeing encompasses a multitude of different spheres of what makes us human.

The World Health Organization defines wellbeing as a 'state of complete physical, mental and social wellbeing and not merely the absence of disease or infirmity'.[7] Similarly, the Victorian government defines wellbeing as 'a complex combination of a person's physical, mental, emotional and social health factors. Wellbeing is strongly linked to happiness and life satisfaction. In short, wellbeing could be described as how you feel about yourself and your life.'[8]

Advancements in how we define wellbeing, how often we talk about it and the focus we give to it have seen a rise in strategies at a personal, organisational and institutional level as to how we obtain wellbeing – or, at least, improve it. Meditation and mindfulness are now more accepted and practised, devices that help us track our steps are worn on our wrists and we're continually encouraged to be informed of what we feed our bodies.

All these personal endeavours to be healthy and well holistically are to be commended and we hope they continue to be implemented. But there is another element at play in our lives that massively impacts our wellbeing and our ability to thrive, and that is *work*. Numerous studies indicate we spend roughly a third of our waking hours at work, which has meant that the focus on wellbeing has now extended to the workplace. There are many books, conferences and seminars that are entirely devoted to helping people better understand how to achieve wellbeing in their lives, and the impact the workplace has on this endeavour.

A foundational element of work wellbeing is workplace safety. The good news in most developed nations and in most industries is that rates of physical injury in the workplace continue to decline. Through better training, technology solutions and heightened employer and worker vigilance, worksites have never been safer. Safe Work Australia data shows that in the latest three-year period, serious workplace incidents have declined by 10%.[9] For many workers, the most dangerous aspect of their job is their daily commute.

At the same time as we have seen safer workplaces physically there has been a growing awareness of the impact of work mentally and emotionally.

Workplace health and safety regimes have robustly turned their attention to mental wellbeing and many organisations have rebranded their workplace health and safety services to *wellbeing* services.

Amid these trends, a growing number of organisations are seeing the value of implementing and encouraging healthy initiatives for their employees. There has been a significant trend in workplaces towards standing desks, natural light and fruit bowls. Our own organisation tries to prioritise the physical and mental health of our team. We encourage walks at lunch time, we have a communal fruit bowl and we (try to) have regular stretch breaks away from our desks. Organisations have realised that having healthy employees' equals having a healthy organisation. They should be recognised and rewarded for this, and we hope these practices and priorities continue to abound.

But as we have pointed out, wellbeing is more than positive physical and mental health. In its holistic definition wellbeing is about our ability as humans to thrive and flourish, and we believe that work plays a crucial role in this. We believe that as humans we are designed to work, that work is good for us, that purposeful work has a positive impact and connects us with others. It is core to our wellbeing and our ability to thrive. Like the growth rings of a tree, our lives can occasionally experience seasons of extraordinary flourishing. We have found three catalysts for such growth: significant adversity, extreme dissatisfaction, or exposure to an exceptional leader.

The concepts we explore in this book are founded on decades of social research and are the culmination of detailed surveys, focus groups and literature reviews into the areas of wellbeing, human thriving and flourishing. We hope it will inform you about the changing nature and context of work, the importance of it in our lives and the opportunity work presents individuals, leaders and organisations to facilitate flourishing workers. In turn, we believe that flourishing workers will contribute to flourishing communities and a flourishing society.

CHAPTER 1

WHAT IS WORK WELLBEING?

When you think about work, how often do you think about it being tied to our human purpose, as a key to flourishing and thriving or as part of the reason for life? This might have been the perspective you held when you first started out in your career, but the longer you've worked the more responsibility you've taken on and perhaps along with this you've taken on more stress. Amid meeting deadlines, leading teams or not getting adequate rest, work has become a burden.

THE ROLE OF WORK IN OUR LIVES

As social researchers we often hold hypotheses about certain topics, then we test them through different research methodologies. One hypothesis we held when writing this book was that people view work as getting in the way of life rather than as being a key part of their life. It's the sentiment of living for the weekend; that work is a hurdle we must get over to get to the good bits; that work is a means to an end. This sentiment is expressed in many ways: in memes that say 'When you haven't even gone to sleep yet and you can't wait to come home from work tomorrow', to bumper stickers on cars that say 'I owe, I owe, I owe, it's off to work I go'.

To test our hypothesis, we surveyed workers by asking them how they felt about their work. Over half of the workers (53%) said they enjoyed work most days. Almost a quarter (23%) said they didn't mind it, and 7% said they hated work. Less than one in five workers (17%) said they loved their work. Clearly work is not universally despised yet less than one in five workers (17%) said they loved their work. These results supported our hypothesis that far too many are not thriving at work. While even those who really enjoy their work might not absolutely love it every single day, it is true that if you love what you do for work you are more likely to be happier and more satisfied and engaged.

In our survey of 1,001 workers across a variety of age groups and industries, we asked the question: *When you wake up on a Monday morning, which of the following best describes how you most commonly feel about the week ahead?* An indefatigable 12% said 'I'm excited and can't wait to get started'; however, more than twice as many (29%) said 'I don't feel great but work is an unavoidable part of life' and a further 6% said 'It's a terrible feeling knowing the working week lies ahead.'

In a follow-up question we asked: *Overall, when you reflect on your work life how do you feel it is going?* A very resilient 9% said 'It is excellent' and another 32% said 'It is very good', but 18% rated it as just 'Fair' and 6% said 'It is poor'. These 6% of workers who feel terrible every Monday morning knowing a work week lies ahead and who rate this key part of their life as 'poor' equate to almost a million workers across Australia and New Zealand, and around 10 million in the United States.

It is important that humans at the very least enjoy, if not love, what they do for work. Work is what we spend the bulk of our life doing, and it contributes to our sense of meaning, purpose and identity in life. It's one avenue that people use to find and build social connections. It's key to our growth as an individual, our development as a person and our contribution to society. We are made to contribute, and work is often the way we grow as leaders and have influence.

While it is true we are defined by more than what we do for work, it is nonetheless an integral part of our identity. When you meet someone at a social gathering one of the first questions often asked is 'What do you do?' or 'Where do you work?' Because work takes up so much of our time it is logical that people might ask this to find out more about who we are. It is an important aspect of our lives and can often be and hopefully is an indicator of our passions, interests and strengths.

The large majority of people will spend a third of their discretionary hours at work, so it's important that whatever we do it's something we enjoy and find purpose in. Steve Jobs, the chairman, chief executive officer and co-founder of Apple Inc., communicated it well when he said: 'Your work is going to fill a large part of your life, and the only way to be truly satisfied is to do what you believe is great work. And the only way to do great work is to love what you do. If you haven't found it yet, keep looking. Don't settle. As with all matters of the heart, you'll know when you find it. And, like any great relationship it just gets better and better as the years roll on. So keep looking until you find it. Don't settle.'

When we feel that our work is purposeful and is having an impact, it often correlates to greater enjoyment in the work. Whatever it is you do for work, no matter how menial or high-flying, we hope you find that it has purpose. During the COVID-19 crisis, despite social isolation policies schools were kept open so that essential workers with children could carry on their jobs. It became clear that essential workers were not just those on the front lines of the pandemic such as health-care workers, but also supermarket workers, transport and supply chain workers and many more. In fact, amid this challenge, the Australian prime minister Scott Morrison championed the importance of all work when he said: 'Everyone who has a job in this economy is an essential worker. Every single job that is being done in our economy is essential.' As Martin Luther King Jr put it, 'If a man is called to be a street sweeper, he should sweep streets even as Michelangelo painted, or Beethoven composed music or Shakespeare wrote poetry. He should sweep streets so well that all the hosts of heaven and earth will pause to say, "Here lived a great street sweeper who did his job well."'

Work plays too big a role in our lives for us to view it as merely a means to an end, as something we have to get through in order to live our best lives. When work is our vocation, when we feel strongly that we are suitable for a particular career or occupation, that's when we will have a greater chance of thriving. This is even more the case with the emerging generations: many young people don't seek a job as much as they seek an opportunity.

WORK IS GOOD FOR US

'Working hard for something we don't care about is called stress; working hard for something we love is called passion.' – Simon Sinek

Can you remember a time when you felt like you were thriving; that you were in the right place at the right time doing the right thing; when you felt alignment to a purpose that increased your sense of meaning or fulfilment? Have you ever been in a place where you described yourself as flourishing?

We believe that work, that businesses, that corporations exist not simply to make money, but to better society in general. And that starts with bettering their teams and increasing their sense of wellbeing. Work is good for us, and organisations and the leaders in them have a unique opportunity to reprioritise the health and wellbeing of their staff.

> **Ashley:** The topic of my keynote presentation at a recent conference concerned the future of work. I spoke about some of the future trends impacting what humans will be doing for work, addressing trends such as automation, robotics and other technological advancements, as well as the demographics that would impact the types of jobs and sectors that will require more workers. The MC at the event was Geniere Aplin, the group executive at workers' compensation firm EML. In her introduction, Geniere spoke about the idea that work is good for us. As I listened to her I found myself agreeing with everything she said. I thanked her at the conclusion of

the event for her perspective on work, mentioning that it was similar to my own.

In ensuing conversations we discussed what the term 'good work' means. Geneire said that the closest she could come to defining good work is:

'having a role or purpose – whether that is voluntary or otherwise – that inspires you to keep going back to that job. It can change over time for people, but it's about being in an environment that supports you delivering positive outcomes. Whether that be making or constructing something and being able to see it at the end of the day. It might be a purpose for people. It's also about having the right tools, the support of whoever you are working for, or the support of your community or the team to deliver that outcome. This makes it good work. I think about it with my daughter and volunteering in the school canteen. It's not something I would normally do but the system of work they had in there and the delegation meant you knew what you were accountable for, what you needed to deliver and when you needed to deliver it by. That support of an organisation in helping define how people do their work and what a good outcome looks like, I think, is critical.'

As futurists we are sometimes asked the questions: 'Do you think we will still be working in, say ten, twenty or thirty years' time?' and 'If robots and artificial intelligence in this fourth industrial revolution can do tasks faster than human beings can, will there be a universal basic income for all people?' Our answer is that, first, while robotics and automation will take over some jobs, new jobs will be created. Second, it is our belief and the basis of many other studies that human beings possess certain skills such as empathy, creativity and context-dependant critical thinking skills that are difficult to translate into a language a computer can understand. Third, and most importantly, work is about more than just earning money: it provides the opportunity for us to make a contribution by using our talents and skills, for social interaction and to find fulfilment in our role. This is why we believe work is something human beings will always do.

While work is designed to be good for us it's evident that some workplaces might not be geared towards allowing their teams to thrive, and that in fact some work environments are toxic or negatively impact people's lives. It would be difficult to acknowledge the positive elements of work when the work environment is not conducive to workers' wellbeing.

Ashley: One of my friends has worked hard all of her life, providing for her family and ensuring her children had opportunities that hadn't been afforded her when she was growing up. She was a hard worker, and aside from her children's younger years she worked her whole life – even during seasons when her husband was out of work and for many years being the main breadwinner. After her children had finished school, moved out of home and got married, she began to transition out of the workforce.

Reflecting on the many years she had worked, she was proud of her contributions. A few months after she had completely transitioned out of the workforce, something heart-wrenching happened: she found out her husband had been having an affair, and he left her. As you can imagine, my friend was absolutely devastated. Not only did she have to confront a life without the person she had been with for 40 years, she had to confront the realities that lay ahead of her; in particular, the financial reality that her retirement was no longer secure and that she would have to go to work again.

A resilient woman, she went job hunting, and it wasn't long before she re-entered the workforce. She told me recently how finding this new role has helped her in ways she didn't expect during one of the darkest periods of her life. Not only had it given her a renewed sense of financial independence, it has also given her purpose and meaning and provided a new community of people. Some of her work colleagues are now her friends. She often tells me that this job, this new work, has helped her through some of the toughest seasons of her life.

DECOUPLING WORK AND EMPLOYMENT

Have you ever thought about what the notion of 'work' means to you: Is it simply a physical place you get paid to go to each day? Is it your passion? Do you dread it? Is it a case of 'I just need to get through this work week so I can get to the weekend'? Is it a means to an end?

In our worker survey we asked the hypothetical question: *'If you won the lottery or received a massive inheritance of several million dollars so that all of your financial needs were taken care of, which of the following best covers what you would do with your current employment situation?'* Exactly half of workers (50%) said they would quit their job. Of those that would, 23% said they would quit the job they are in and never work again. The remaining 27% said they would quit their current job and find other work. The other 50% would stay in their current role. Of those, a third (33%) would stay in their current role but would cut down the days, and 17% said they would stay in their current role unchanged.

Another question asked how workers feel about their work, with 17% saying they loved it. It is likely this group are the same ones who would stay in their current role unchanged. If work is good for us, if it provides benefits beyond financial reward and contributes to our sense of purpose and meaning, accomplishment and relationships and sense of community, then why is it that for half of all workers work has become a burden?

Part of the reason for this is that the role of work in our lives has changed. Today, 'work' has become synonymous with 'employment'. The definition of employment is 'the state of having paid work', whereas the definition of work is 'activity involving mental or physical effort done in order to achieve a purpose or result'. These definitions are vastly different, yet we tend to jumble them together. We've made work about success, status, power and money, when the true essence of work is about contributing and making an impact.

People can 'work' without having an employment contract and without being paid, as do millions of people around the world. There are 2.9 million Australian volunteers and over three million stay-at-home parents. Our research shows that grandparents are increasingly taking an active carer role with their grandchildren and helping out with their activities. The foundation of our communities are sporting clubs, membership associations, churches and other local organisations, all of which are sustained by the work of volunteers. These volunteers are working but are not being remunerated for it. They are not 'employed' but they are making a difference, fulfilling a purpose and helping communities and individuals. They are 'working'. We even see this being played out in our youngest generations: have you ever seen a child play with their toys?

> **Mark:** As adults, we can dismiss the activities of children simply as play, yet when I watch my youngest son Corban spend hours building little worlds with blocks, I can see it is more akin to work than play. He expends much effort on his envisioned purpose, but it is a creative, fun and engaging pursuit (much like work should be) and he is working towards a result. This is not just meaningless play, and I see this clearly from his response when one of his siblings knocks his world over!

The concentration and effort children display when pursing their selected outcome, whether it's playing a game, making a craft or setting up cars, blocks or dolls, is remarkable. Why? Because they care about achieving an outcome, the finished product, and in their mind they are working towards it. Yes, they are playing, but it's not just playing: they are also working. As

Alan Watts put it: 'This is the real secret of life – to be completely engaged with what you are doing in the here and now. And instead of calling it work, realize it is play.'

The concept of work starts young, without us being aware of it; it doesn't just start when teenagers turn 14 and nine months and begin paid employment at McDonald's. We work at things our whole life, from building a Lego bridge to studying for an exam or training for a sporting match. All of this is work, and often we don't do it alone as it's frequently in the company of others.

Many people would consider themselves to be employed by a 'company', the dictionary definition for which is 'an entity that engages in business'. However, the origins of the word suggest a deeper meaning as it comes from the Latin *companio*, or 'companion'. The *com* in companion means 'with', while *panis* is the Latin word for 'bread' or 'food'. In that root you can identify the basis on which the notion of companionship originally hinged: a companion was one with whom you ate a meal.[1] Thus in the word 'company', literally 'together breaking bread', we have a link between people working and sharing together for a common output.

A company of people today often comprises much diversity: in gender, generation, cultural background, opinion, perspective and life experience, to name a few. Yet despite these differences a company of people work towards a unified goal and purpose. When unity is created among diversity, when we celebrate alignment to a clear goal or vision, we open the door not only to success and achievement but also to wellbeing.

Over time, the changing concept of work has left economists, investors and big corporates with the perspective that profit and the resulting shareholder return is the raison d'être. However, from its origins capitalism has always focused on the customer and the common good. A key feature of capitalism is that it is a multiplier of money: shareholders grow their investments, customers receive good value on their exchange, the company pays earnings to staff members and in addition the capital value of the business increases. Yet the beauty of a virtuous business is not only that it creates monetary value but that it creates a flourishing cycle of wellbeing.

Australian economist Ian Harper is the dean of Melbourne Business School and co-dean of the University of Melbourne's Faculty of Business and Economics. He is known for his work in public policy, and in May 2016 was appointed to the board of the Reserve Bank of Australia and became a senior adviser to Deloitte Access Economics, having previously been a partner with the firm. When interviewing him about the role of work in our lives, Ian said he believes that:

> Work is about human fulfilment and purpose. We were made to work as it expresses our humanness. But there is a distinction between work and drudgery. I don't think people were made to be drudges. And when people think about work in a sort of simplistic context, within an economist's frame, it's often thought about as exactly that: work as disutility or drudgery. But even economists know that that's not true. We work because it fulfils our purpose and is part of what gives us a sense of meaning.
>
> Now, if I start to think about work in that characteristic way, then what I say about wages becomes more complex. Work is becoming far more varied in the tasks people are asked to perform and the autonomy that people have. It includes what your colleagues are doing, who your colleagues are, when you are on the job, when you're not and where you work. And what this makes for is increasingly stimulating, encouraging, creative work. So when people think about an opportunity to work, they increasingly think through the different dimensions like whether they will have to move, if they'll have to do shiftwork every fourth week – a whole raft of different things. And the employer, therefore, has pressure applied to start thinking about these things.
>
> At the end of the day, any business that wants productive and creative talent knows it comes bundled up with all sorts of emotions and other commitments, and [as the employer]

I need to find a way to induce you [my staff] to give me your best or as much of your creative talent as you're prepared to, to engage with my wider purpose. And I need you to do that willingly. Because if this is against your will you're not going to do it, you're going to withhold, there'll be no discretionary effort, and you'll go through the motions. I won't get what I'm really looking for, which is that creative spark, that excitement, until I create the environment. And all of that is far richer than suggesting that work is just about drudgery. On the other hand, money does have an impact, but it's not always the first thing people consider. So it comes down to the fact that the models need to be richer to get a fuller understanding of why people work and what draws them in. So I think a lot of that boils down to the fact that economists clearly are aware that there are many more dimensions to the work/leisure decision than the traditional simple models would imply.

One of the key reasons that people work is to earn a living, but as Ian points out it is not the only reason. When work is good for us, when both employers and employees view it as more than just a job or place of employment, it creates an environment for people's wellbeing to be prioritised and valued.

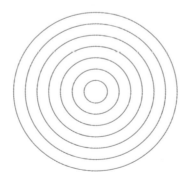

'Many young
people don't seek
a job as much
as they seek an
opportunity.'

– McCRINDLE

WELLBEING AT WORK

Achieving wellbeing in both personal and work spheres has been a goal for human existence, even as far back as Aristotle's day. He said: 'Pleasure in the job puts perfection in the work.'

In a McCrindle survey of 1,160 working Australians, we asked the question: *'How important are the following elements in your workplace?'* We had respondents evaluate 17 different elements specific to the workplace in terms of importance. Workplace wellbeing ranked as the most important element, with 72% of respondents rating this as extremely or very important to them. This ranked above other workplace elements such as relationship with peers/colleagues (65%), a collaborative work environment (60%), flexible working hours (60%) and inspiring, accessible leadership (58%).

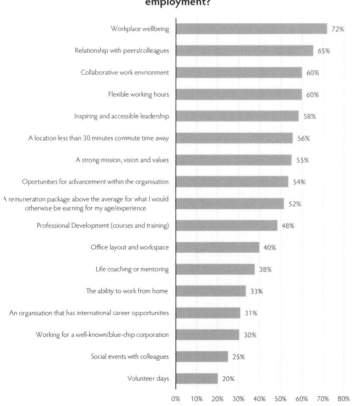

How important are the following elements in your place of employment?

Have you ever thought about how you define wellbeing? Do you incorporate physical and mental health along with human flourishing and thriving?

According to a study of employed Australians conducted by McCrindle and Reventure,[2] the majority of workers (42%) defined wellbeing as 'when I have found balance across my physical, mental, social and spiritual life'. A third (33%) of respondents said wellbeing was 'when I feel physically and mentally fit and well', 13% said it's 'when I have found inner peace' and 12% said it's 'when my desires for house/income/success are met'.

Esteemed psychologist, educator and author Martin Seligman is well known for his theories of positive psychology and wellbeing. In his book *Flourish*, Seligman delves into the difference between authentic happiness and wellbeing: 'I used to think that the topic of positive psychology was happiness, that the gold standard of measuring happiness was life satisfaction, and that the goal of positive psychology was to increase life satisfaction. I now think that the topic of positive psychology is wellbeing, that the gold standard for measuring wellbeing is flourishing, and that the goal of positive psychology is to increase flourishing.'[3]

He goes on to say that 'wellbeing is just like "weather" and "freedom" in its structure: no single measure defines it exhaustively, but several things contribute to it: these are the elements of wellbeing, and each of the elements is a measurable thing.' The five elements Seligman notes as contributing to wellbeing are positive emotion, engagement, meaning and purpose, positive relationships and accomplishment.[4]

When thinking about this idea of flourishing Seligman cites Felicia Huppert and Timothy So of the University of Cambridge, who defined flourishing as 'having all the core features (positive emotions, engagement, interest, meaning and purpose) as well as three of the additional features (self-esteem, optimism, resilience, vitality, self-determination and positive relationships)'.[5] When it comes to personal wellbeing, this refers to factors that individuals can control such as sleep, sense of satisfaction, sense of meaning and purpose, feelings or emotions and how one feels their life is going. Holistically it incorporates the physical, mental, emotional and spiritual. It's personal.

Another recent report states that flourishing and thriving at work are about helping employees to:

* ❖ strengthen their personal resources
* ❖ flourish and take pride in their role within the organisational system
* ❖ function to the best of their abilities, both as individuals and in collaboration with their colleagues
* ❖ have a positive overall experience of work.[6]

Taking all of this into consideration, *work* wellbeing is bigger than *workplace* wellbeing; it is bigger than fruit bowls, standing desks and other practices that help people to feel less stressed and more valued. These initiatives are important, but an approach to work wellbeing needs to be more than these tangible features. It needs to be a mindset, a set of values and practices shared by leaders and teams. It needs to be more integrated and holistic, not just tokenistic.

Work wellbeing exists where people are championed above profits, where the culture is aspirational and inspirational not just transactional, where leaders are focused on creating a community of customers, clients and teams and where there is a compelling passion for societal good rather than personal gain.

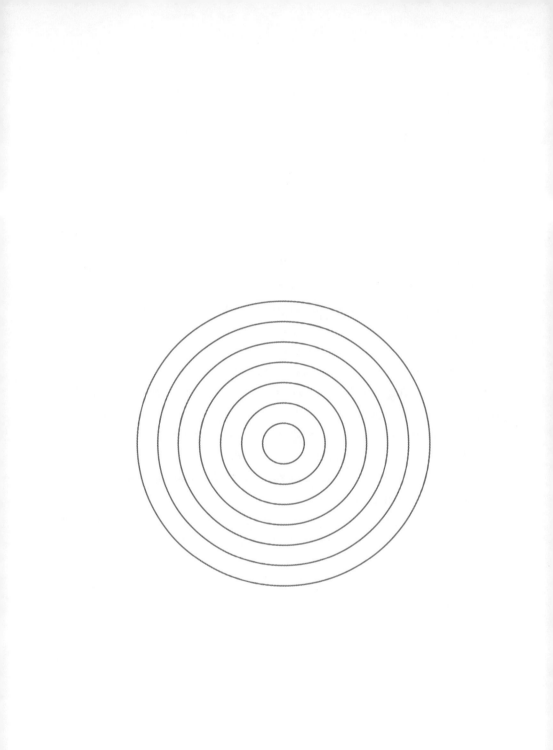

CHAPTER 2

THE FUTURE
OF WORK

It is undisputed that the world of work is undergoing a massive transformation: from artificial intelligence to robotics and automation, what humans currently do and will be doing for work in the future is changing. The World Economic Forum predicts that '65% of children entering primary school today will ultimately end up working in completely new job types that don't yet exist'.[1] From the gig economy to teleworking and portfolio careers, how, where and why we work is changing.

It is not only technological shifts that are having big impacts on the workforce. Although they redefine our world, social and demographic changes also have profound implications for our future.

One of the key definers of 21st-century workplaces is *diversity*. There are more women in the workforce now than there has ever been due to redefined life stages, the cost of living and advances in gender roles. As well, workplaces are now increasingly generationally and culturally diverse.

Workers expect their organisations to reflect the broader society in which they operate, which is particularly true for the emerging Generation Z's, who have been shaped in an era of much cultural and gender diversity and respond well to generational diversity. For a large proportion of Generation Z, their leader being born outside of Australia, their leader being a woman and their leader being the same age as them makes no difference (75, 67 and 66% respectively). And the majority of those who didn't select 'makes no difference' actually stated that those characteristics in leaders are positives.

The benefits of diversity (age, gender, cultural background and so on) in the demographics of a workplace as well as in other differences (personal characteristics, family composition, education, tenure within a company or lifestyle) enable organisations to create a competitive advantage for themselves. By welcoming different perspectives, they are better able to connect with a wider and more global audience.

EML executive Geniere Aplin believes organisations have some way to go in achieving this sort of diversity. When asked how workplaces are going in the area of diversity and employees thriving at work, she said: 'I would probably say not as well as we would like to be, or not as well as I'd like us to be. For the reason that board tables and leadership are not particularly diverse. When you've got people who have generally attended the same school, the same universities and perhaps never had any financial sufferings, it's very difficult to create an environment or products for the customer that truly serve or create wellness in people.'

When people feel as though they don't belong in a community or workplace they can experience a sense of 'onlyness'. McKinsey & Company noted that 20% of women experience an 'only' moment when they are the only female in a room.[2] For women of colour the number rose to 45%; for men it was just 7%. Women are more likely to experience discrimination in the workplace than men, but being the only woman is even more discomfiting and has far-reaching effects.

Solitary females in a workplace are more likely to: have their judgement questioned than women working in a gender-balanced environment (49% cf. 32%); be mistaken for someone more junior (35% cf. 15%); and be subjected to unprofessional and demeaning remarks (24% cf. 14%). The research also discovered the concerning reality that women who experience onlyness are more likely to contemplate leaving their jobs (26%) than other women (17%).[3]

But diversity in and of itself is not the goal: inclusivity is. When people of diverse backgrounds feel united and aligned to a bigger purpose and that the environment is one in which it is safe to contribute diverse ideas, employees can thrive – and so in turn can the organisation. According to Gallup: 'Employees who feel they can be themselves in the workplace have been found to be more engaged and have higher self-reported performance than employees who feel otherwise.'[4]

GENDER DIVERSITY

Due to the rising cost of living, many households need a dual income. Additionally, the emerging generations are delaying the traditional life markers of marriage and having children and, with more Generation Z's going to university than did previous generations, many young people are starting their earning years in debt. These social shifts have resulted in more women being in the workforce now than at any other time in history. Although women comprise almost exactly half (47%) of Australia's workforce, only 17% are CEOs and 30% directors in the ASX 200 companies.[5] Wellbeing will be enhanced in our workplaces as these percentages grow so that eventually organisations, boards and governance will be reflective of the society in which they operate.

Australians are positive about women being in leadership and senior roles. Three in four employed Australians (74%) consider equal representation of women on company boards and in corporate leadership to be important, yet 48% believe not enough progress is being made towards this ambition.

More than two in five employed Australians (44%) either strongly or at least somewhat agree that not having adequate flexible working options holds back Australian workplaces from achieving 50% women in senior leadership roles, followed by a lack of support for women exiting the workplace for family reasons (41% strongly or somewhat agree). If we want more women in the workforce we need more organisations to model flexibility and wellbeing that enables women and parents generally to thrive in the workforce while juggling competing priorities.

In her book *Thrive*, founder of the Huffington Post Arianna Huffington said: 'Most of the time, the discussion about the challenges of women at the top centres around the difficulty of navigating career and children – of "having it all". It's time we recognise that, as the workplace is currently structured, a lot of women don't want to get to the top and stay there because they don't want to pay the price – in terms of their health, their wellbeing and their happiness.'[6]

Flexible workplace conditions are critical to overall employee engagement, and not just for women. When speaking about her own leadership style, Geniere Aplin said: 'I'm fairly flexible with my direct reports in the way they work because I know them all really well and I trust their output. I still encounter people in my generation who think you must be in the office from seven am to seven pm to be doing the job or to get promoted. That doesn't create well people or people who have a full sense of life. From my perspective, I'd like to become more active around thinking about work wellness and good work, particularly as we move towards looking at flexible work more often.'

To ensure women have the same opportunities as their male counterparts, 21st-century workplaces need to prioritise flexibility to allow for both mums and dads to thrive in their career. The emerging generation of workers are post-dialectic in their nature, seeking both career advancement and a family. Women have a tremendous capacity to juggle various commitments – albeit not without challenges – but to allow for this increasing need organisations need to provide flexibility and support for both men and women along with leaders who model this well. Many organisations have implemented practical strategies to achieve this such as flexible working hours, job sharing and tracking opportunities, extended parental leave, teleworking options, senior leaders modelling healthy work-life balance, shared leadership roles and a tracking metrics of wellbeing in addition to performance. An aspirational workplace requires leaders to be an example of what others aspire to be; you can't be what you can't see.

GENERATIONAL DIVERSITY

In recent times the realities of massive generational change have dawned on business leaders. While the issues of an ageing population and a new attitude to work have been emerging for some time, for many organisations it has been a sudden awakening. Dealing with these demographic changes and specifically how to recruit, retain and manage staff has become one of the biggest issues now facing employers.

Like many other nations, Australia's population is growing at an unprecedented rate, yet we are also experiencing a rapid ageing of the population. By the mid-2030s it is predicted there will be more people aged over 65 than under 18 for the first time in Australian history.

Nowhere are the implications of this more significant than in employment. An ageing population leads directly to an ageing workforce, and in the coming years Australia's working-age population (ages 15 to 64) is projected to decline as a proportion of the total population.[7]

A larger proportion of the older generations will remain in the workforce for longer, while the oldest of the Generation Z's (those born between 1995 and 2009) form the newest cohort of employees and are transforming the dynamics.

As of 2020 there were more Australians born since 1980 than before it, meaning that Generation Y (born from 1980 to 1994), Generation Z and Generation Alpha (born since 2010) comprised over half of the population. Additionally, from 2019 Generation Y and Generation Z comprised the majority of the workforce, outnumbering Generation X and Baby Boomers for the first time. This shift means that Generation Y and Generation Z also dominate as consumers and new household formers and therefore are a key demographic with which to engage.

To achieve effective and sustainable work wellbeing we need to understand the attitudinal shifts, social trends and mindset of the ever-changing customer and employee.

Talking about your generation

It is essential for today's leaders to understand and then engage with the people within their communities, whether this be in a workplace context or otherwise, as it is essential to facilitate wellbeing. If leaders don't do this they will edge towards irrelevancy. Stephen Covey, the author of *The 7 Habits of Highly Effective People*, said: 'If I were to summarize in one sentence the single most important principle I have learned in the field of interpersonal relations, it would be this: Seek first to understand, then to be understood.'[8] So who comprises the different generations, and how are they defined?

These are the current generations:

- ❖ Builders, born from 1925 to 1945

- ❖ Baby Boomers, born from 1946 to 1964

- ❖ Generation X, born from 1965 to 1979

- ❖ Generation Y, born from 1980 to 1994

- ❖ Generation Z, born from 1995 to 2009

- ❖ Generation Alpha, born from 2010 to 2024 (with Generation Beta to follow, born from 2025)

Defining the generations: from biology to sociology

A generation has been defined as the interval of time between the birth of parents and the birth of their children. Traditionally this places a generation at around 25 years in span and, while in the past this has served sociologists well when analysing generations, for several reasons it is irrelevant today.

First, cohorts are changing quickly in response to new technologies, modifying careers and study options. Shifting societal values mean two decades is far too broad to contain all the people born within this time span.

Second, the time between the birth of parents and the birth of their offspring has stretched out from two decades to more than three. In 1976 the median age of a woman having her first baby was 24, whereas now it is just over 31.[9]

These two factors have contributed to a move away from a biological definition to a sociological one. Today, a generation refers to a cohort of people born and shaped by a span of time, that span of time having contracted significantly from 20 years to 15 years. While some argue 15 years is too long, if the span were any shorter we would have too many generations and it would be nonsense to discuss. The 15-year time span is long enough to include a period that shapes formative years, but not so long that it becomes meaningless. It encompasses the natural flow of social change yet is not too long to include entire cycles of cultural change.

Naming and labelling generations

Every generation since the Baby Boomers spans 15 years regardless of events and circumstances. They are also labelled using letters (X, Y, Z and Alpha and Beta), which is a more scientific approach to categorisation. Having a set and consistent timespan (15 years) allows for more useful comparisons. There are many variables across the generations, but keeping a constant of birth span is a helpful modification of this field of generational analysis.

There have been other attempts to label generations, 'Millennials' being one example. The problem with this label is that it defines that generation around a single event (the start of the new millennium) and creates a vague birth range. Were the Millennials born from the 1980s in the lead up to the new millennium or were they born in the first decade of this millennium?

The label also colours the analysis. 'Millennials' seems a misfit in labelling people born 20 years before the new millennium and even more anachronistic now, more than 20 years into the new millennium. And 'Baby Boomers' seems odd for a generation in which the oldest are now entering their seventies. Using a set span of birth years and a non-descriptive label allows objective analysis for each generation. A label such as Generation Z provides a blank canvas on which a generation can create its own identity and is preferred over a descriptive label that is relevant for just a segment of the cohort or for a period of time. It will also allow for greater analysis and global comparisons.

This sociological as opposed to pop-culture approach to generational analysis is set to continue for the generations to come. The new cohort is Generation Alpha, those born from 2010 to 2024.[10] Generation Beta will comprise those born from 2025 to 2039 and will be followed by Generation Gamma.

Baby Boomers

The Baby Boomers have lived through incredible change, adapting to and even creating the change. They are therefore a very flexible generation, which is demonstrated in everything from their embrace of technology to their collaborative management style. Members of this generation are likely to remain in leadership positions for longer than any previous generation. Their experience combined with their adaptivity will keep them relevant, so it's important that we don't apply our 20th-century perceptions of age to the 21st-century 'younger longer' Baby Boomers. For them, age really is just a number.

Generation X

Generation X is the perfect bridge generation, as they understand and usually adopt the work ethic and focus of the Boomers.

Generation X began their economic life when jobs were harder to get and keep. The early 1990s witnessed a recession and downsizing of the workforce, which was very different to the near-full employment we enjoyed for almost three decades until the COVID-19 impacts. Generation X are close in age to the Generation Ys and can connect somewhat with their culture, views and even values.

Generation Y

While derided as fickle, self-focused and transient, the reality is that those comprising Generation Y have invested significantly in their education and are committed to growing their careers. They are the generation who largely began their working life in the post-GFC environment and began their family-forming years in the COVID-19 context. Far from being the 'snowflake generation', as some disparagingly labelled them, it turns out they are generation resilient.

If leaders can step out from behind the corporate image, build staff rapport and relate to individuals, they will get loyalty and commitment from Generation Y.

Generation Z

Generation Z is almost exclusively the children of Generation X and are powerful players in today's work culture. With a lifetime of experience in online learning and social connecting through technology platforms, working remotely came naturally to them. Some had playfully called them 'Zoomers', and when Zoom became the new platform for work meetings and classroom interaction this generation gave new meaning to that label. While Generation Z now comprises one in seven workers, by 2030 they will comprise a third of the workforce and will be an important demographic to engage with.

Generation Alpha

The world saw the start of a new generation from 2010. In the mid-2000s, when we were looking into the emerging generations, we realised that no one had given much thought to what the generation after Generation Z would be called. We conducted a survey to find out what people thought the next generation should be called and naturally most people responded with the suggestion 'Generation A', having completed the alphabet with Generation Z.

This generation is the first to be fully born in the 21st century so we decided to name them Generation Alpha, moving to the beginning of the Greek alphabet to signify not a return to the old but the start of something new. Generation Alpha began the same year the first iPad was released, Instagram was launched and 'app' was named word of the year. Consequently, they have been labelled as digital integrators, the iGen and Generation Glass, with technology having been seamlessly integrated into their lives from their first years.

Generation Alpha are the children of Generation Y, while their grandparents are younger Boomers. Based on the length of a generation being 15 years, Generation Alpha will be complete by 2025, from when we will commence Generation Beta.

By 2030, Generation Alpha will comprise one in 10 workers. This generation will come of age in a time of unprecedented ageing, rising costs, emerging global challenges and the biggest intergenerational transfer of wealth and leadership succession ever seen. Generation Alpha will surpass even the praised and sophisticated Zeds in terms of education, with university education predicted to be more common among this generation than in any previous generation.

Effects of generational diversity

Clearly there are many differences between the generations, although youth of all eras demonstrate some similar characteristics such as experimental lifestyles, questioning the status quo, idealism and pushing the boundaries. However, you would not say that those who grew up in the 1970s were the same as those who came of age in the 1990s or those who are coming of age today, yet sometimes we are asked the question: 'Are the generations really *that* different?' Some people hold the perspective that 'Generation Z is just a label; they're the same as the young people of my day.' We believe that generations do not morph over time to being identical in character to how their parents were at the same age, but rather that a generation is a product of their current age, their times and, importantly, the formative technologies and social markers that uniquely shaped them. As history has consistently shown, people resemble their times more than they resemble their parents.

Social events such as World War II, the moon landing, the stock market crash, September 11, the GFC, Donald Trump's election as president of the United States, Brexit and COVID-19 have all been defining moments in modern history that have had different impacts on each generation depending on the age people were when they took place. The same can be said for the introduction of transformative technology such as the television, personal computers and the internet. All of these events and technologies defined and in some cases significantly impacted each generation.

Ashley: Like many people across the world, I remember exactly where I was and what I was doing the moment I found out about the September 11 attacks. As a Generation Y this event is often identified as being a key defining moment in history for my generation. My mum can say the same about the moon landing: she remembers exactly where she was and what she was doing when this important moment in history took place. My mum also remembers the first time she watched something in colour TV, while I remember getting my first-ever iPhone. While age influences behaviour and attitudes, greater impacts are made by the culture in which we live out our youth and by significant events that took place during our formative years.

As Australians live longer and work later in life, we will have a more diverse mix of generations interacting in our workplaces. Having this mix in the workplace is nothing new, although older people have traditionally been in senior managerial positions while younger people worked the front desk, on the factory floor or out in the field. Not so today. The new reality is one where teams of diverse ages work together on a project, where older leaders give guidance across several generations and where young graduates engage with and lead older workers.

According to a Deloitte report about the evolution of work and the new realities facing leaders: 'Lifelong reinvention can be enhanced by leveraging the strengths of each generation. There is an implied assumption that all future young workers would bring to the workplace superb skills. The reality might be different. It might be that the value of older workers might actually improve, not for their productivity, but rather as role models for their work ethics. The use of mentoring models is likely to rise in this new reality, with older workers teaching early career workers interpersonal and leadership skills, which often develop with experience.'[11]

In our interviews with workplace and business leaders, many said that mentoring was a key component of creating thriving workplace cultures. John Anderson, former deputy prime minister of Australia and leader of the National Party from 1999 to 2005, said in an interview that in his experience 'There are many young people who are really, deeply interested in being well mentored by older folk, and they need to be. Wherever there is an opportunity for us to be a listening ear that encourages, we should consciously seek to respond.'

Mentoring is a great vehicle for values sharing and transferring knowledge between the different generations. In his book *Chapter One* Daniel Flynn, co-founder of the social enterprise Thankyou, said:

> Here's something you probably didn't know: mentoring is the only proven form of time travel you can readily access. This is what I love about great mentors: they don't do it to be recognised. They do it because they genuinely believe in you and want to see you go further than they've ever gone. They are selflessly willing to gift you pearls of wisdom and advice that may have taken them a lifetime of experience to build. Their secret weapon is that they can help shift your perspective, without you even realising a change in perspective was needed.
>
> There is a satisfaction that arises when you know that your life's work, your journey, your lessons learned could go on to help propel someone else's journey. There is satisfaction in seeing a younger person or someone that is less experienced reach their full potential and at the same time, know that you've been able to play a small part in that journey. Thankyou is where it is today because of the dozens of mentors who have believed in me, challenged me, refined me and encouraged me and helped change my perspective.[12]

Rather than just applying the traditional 'older manager mentors' younger employee', try reverse mentoring and have the knowledge flow both ways. Let the older share experience and expertise while the younger give insights into engaging with their generation, the new times and technologies.

Acknowledging that different generations bring different strengths and challenges to the workplace regarding communication and leadership styles is the first step in creating an engaging culture. Workplaces or communities where people feel safe to contribute new ideas, feel like they belong and like they are a valued part of the team are all indicators of healthy wellbeing and contribute to people's ability to thrive.

CULTURAL DIVERSITY

Another element of diversity in the workplace is that our communities are more culturally varied, which is truer of Australia than of any other developed nation on the planet, with migration being a key driver of population growth. Three in 10 Australians (29%) were born overseas – that's twice the proportion of overseas-born residents in the US (14%) and the UK (14%).[13]

Never before has the workforce been more global. Employers routinely hire staff from abroad and the emerging generation of workers think beyond country borders when considering study, work or business opportunities. In an era of video conferencing and teleworking, it is not unusual for managers to be leading team members located in different countries.

In response to a more diverse workforce, we need greater emotional intelligence (EQ), cultural intelligence (CQ) and generational intelligence (GQ). Our survey of workers supports this, with 72% saying EQ is extremely or very important, and 71% saying regular intelligence is extremely or very important for managers to possess. Additionally, GQ is considered extremely or very important by 67% of workers, as is CQ (62% consider this to be extremely or very important for a manger to possess in the workplace). Leaders need these skills to bridge gaps and create cohesion and a common direction among diverse teams.

SMALL BUSINESSES

Australia has always been an entrepreneurial nation, with small businesses providing the backbone of the economy and the labour force. The spirit of independence, a DIY attitude and the courage to give things a go are strongly demonstrated, with 99.8% of all businesses considered to be small to medium in size. Three in five businesses (61%) are non-employing, with 98% of all businesses employing less than 20 people. It is most common for an employing business to employ between one and four employees, this size making up 72% of employing businesses.[14]

When we asked the question: *'When thinking about mental health issues in Australia today, work-related stress and workplace-related conflict, to what extent do you think employers have a responsibility to ensure wellbeing among their staff?'*, more than four in five (83%) thought that workplace wellbeing, like workplace safety, was essential for employers to ensure, compared to just 4% who thought wellbeing was largely or totally the responsibility of the employee. Just 13% said that ensuring employee wellbeing was the responsibility of both employee and the employer. Although small businesses comprise the majority of employing businesses, it is essential that organisations of all sizes prioritise the wellbeing of their teams. Refer to Chapter 3 for further information.

THE WORK 'PLACE'

When it comes to work and leading teams that thrive, the world in which leaders need to do this is undergoing some seismic shifts. From portfolio careers to remote working, from the gig economy to the growth of the start-up culture, how, where and why we work has significantly changed.

COVID-19 necessitated the most transformational shifts to work for perhaps a century. The most notable was when almost overnight the office-bound workforce globally relocated to their homes. For the first time in modern history working from home became the norm and even ushered in the three letter acronym to describe it: WFH. The technology each of us has access to and the connectivity provided by collaborative platforms and video conferencing meant that many businesses could continue their operations without any staff in their office. Our national survey amid the COVID-19 crisis showed that 69% were as, if not more, productive when working from home than they were at their office. This research also showed that far from being a temporary response to a global pandemic, 78% believed that working from home will become the new normal. There has already been a challenge for leaders to ensure the wellbeing of their staff when they gather in their physical office. This is an even greater challenge when staff are operating remotely from their individual places of residence. The challenge of increased screen time, sedentary lives and social isolation was a growing problem we identified even before the COVID-19 crisis. Almost two in five Australian workers (38%) spend more time in front of a screen at their workplace than they did 12 months ago. One in three workers (33%) spend more time working individually on projects, and almost one in three (31%) spend more time working outside of their usual business hours than they were 12 months ago.[15] Digital technologies and a global workforce are blurring the lines of work and rest, enabling people to work anywhere at any time. This in turn is making it harder for workers to detach themselves from their work and can have a negative impact on work/life balance.

The gig economy and precarious work (non-standard employment) are also impacting where and when people work. The fastest growing employment type is 'non-fulltime'. One in three 18-29 year olds have a 'side hustle' outside their normal job.[16] However a McCrindle report in partnership with Reventure revealed that more than two in five workers (45%) felt insecure about their current workplace arrangement. The greatest perceived benefit of the casualisation of the Australian workforce was flexibility (42%), but the greatest risk of casualisation for individuals was financial instability (59%), the lack of leave benefits (59%) and the unpredictable hours, leading to a decrease in workers' ability to commit (57%).[17] While the gig economy can provide greater choice and flexibility for workers, clearly it can also negatively impact on workers' wellbeing if they do not feel secure in their work.

While workers want flexible working hours as an option, the downside is that as work becomes more precarious isolated workers miss out on the collaboration that comes from working with a team of people. This extends to our workplaces, with face-to-face interaction and interpersonal interactions becoming increasingly rare as devices become more ingrained in people's lives. As a result, what we are seeing is an increase in workplace loneliness, with 37% of people feeling lonely at work.[18]

The emerging generation are the most technologically savvy generation of workers ever seen. They have been shaped in the digital era and have only ever known the world of smart phones, apps and social media. They are using technology in very productive ways, but they also have been best placed to witness the downsides of technology and how screen time and social media can diminish rather than enhance community. The Deloitte Millennials survey shows that while this generation is warm towards technology and its productivity, they are more negative than positive when it comes to the impact it is having on making workplaces less human. More than half of those surveyed (53%) said they were pessimistic about technology's impact, particularly around a diminishing culture that enables social interaction.[19] The changing nature of work, along with what the work*place* looks like, means workplace leaders need to adjust and adapt their strategies about how, where and when they will prioritise work wellbeing.

CHAPTER 3

WHY WORK
WELLBEING MUST
BE THE KEY ISSUE

There are many reasons why work wellbeing needs to be at the top of the agendas of workplace leaders. Western culture faces significant health concerns from people being overworked, stressed and burnt out, which not only impacts people's personal health and ability to thrive, it can also lead to increased absenteeism, presenteeism and decreased productivity. All of these issues will affect an organisation's ability to perform well.

David Cameron, the United Kingdom's prime minister from 2010 to 2016, highlighted the importance of wellbeing at a Google Zeitgeist Europe conference in 2006. He said: 'It's time we admitted that there's more to life than money, and it's time we focused not just on GDP, but on GWB – general wellbeing. Wellbeing can't be measured by money or traded in markets. It's about the beauty of our surroundings, the quality of our culture and, above all, the strength of our relationships.'

Five decades earlier, Robert Kennedy also highlighted the comprehensiveness along with the very obvious deficiencies of national economic measures in his oft-quoted University of Kansas address on 18 March 1968:

> The gross national product does not allow for the health of our children, the quality of their education or the joy of their play. It does not include the beauty of our poetry or the strength of our marriages, the intelligence of our public debate or the integrity of our public officials. It measures neither our wit nor our courage, neither our wisdom nor our learning, neither our compassion nor our devotion to our country. It measures everything, in short, except that which makes life worthwhile.

World leaders have of recent times made efforts to better measure and focus on national wellbeing and not just national wealth. The UK now publishes a national wellbeing dashboard that measures national wellbeing across 10 areas such as health, relationships, personal wellbeing, education, environment and so on.

In 2019 the New Zealand government released their first (and a world first) wellbeing budget, where the traditional budget process was revised to integrate community wellbeing at its core. The budget was aligned around five key areas that included economic categories such as building productivity and transforming the economy with others such as mental health, child wellbeing and supporting Maori and Pacific Islander peoples.

In 1998 the World Health Organization published their first wellbeing index,[1] a five item questionnaire that has been clinically shown to be a valid measure of individual wellbeing. Respondents rated each of the following statements based on the previous two weeks, where 0 = at no time, 1 = some of the time, 2 = less than half of the time, 3 = more than half of the time and 4 = most of the time:

- ❖ I have felt cheerful and in good spirits

- ❖ I have felt calm and relaxed

- ❖ I have felt active and vigorous

- ❖ I woke up feeling fresh and rested

- ❖ My daily life has been filled with things that interest me

The total raw score, ranging from 0 to 25, is multiplied by four to give the final score, with 0 representing the worst imaginable wellbeing and 100 representing the best imaginable wellbeing. The final score can then be benchmarked against the following scale:

- ❖ 80-100 outstanding

- ❖ 65-80 normal to above average

- ❖ 50-65 normal to below average

- ❖ 28-50 reduced wellbeing

- ❖ 0-28 high risk for mental illness

Over the last few decades the focus wellbeing has been given in our personal and professional lives has increased, and it's not hard to see why. If people's wellbeing is not prioritised it has negative implications at both individual and organisational levels, giving rise to the toxic results of stress on increasing mental health issues and higher employee turnover.

WORK AS THE THIRD PLACE

Historically, the 'third place' refers to social settings that are separate from the two usual social environments: home (first place) and the workplace (second place). Traditionally, examples of third-place environments would be churches, libraries, parks or cafes.

The long-time CEO of Starbucks, Howard Schultz, famously set the vision of making their stores the third place. The Starbucks third place policy begins: 'We want our stores to be the third place, a warm and welcoming environment where customers can gather and connect.'

This vision has become a reality not just for Starbucks but for many thousands of cafes and eateries worldwide that are full of people using laptops, smartphones and books, not necessarily connecting with those around them but vicariously experiencing community connection in a busy, fragmented world.

Living in the 'great screen age', in which we spend more time on our devices than in face-to-face interaction, most of us are less likely to be involved with traditional community groups or activities. This is particularly the case for emerging generations, who have been more shaped by digital devices and are delaying traditional life markers such as getting married and having children.

Not only have careers morphed and evolved, but the role of work in our lives is also less isolated than it used to be. While work does blur with life, the expectations we bring to work are not just a fair day's work for a fair day's pay. It's now also about social needs, self-actualisation and the contribution we can make to our community. As a result, we are seeing the workplace not only be the second space but the third place as well.

This idea of work as the 'third place' has given rise to a range of workplace initiates, from wellbeing programs to volunteer opportunities, daily mindfulness, breakout rooms, ping pong tables and social events. While social activities used to take place on a Friday night after work, the workplace of today is a combination of work, social and health-related priorities. After-work drinks have morphed into more integrated and inclusive social engagement practices, which is important in an era when workers look to have multiple needs met at work. Sure, it's about achieving task outcomes and receiving financial rewards, but it's also about social connection, training, personal development, greater fulfilment and even environmental sustainability.

With work becoming the third place, work wellbeing needs to be the key issue for two reasons. Because people are spending so much time at work the workplace itself needs to be geared up to enable people to flourish and thrive when they are there. Also, because work is replacing more traditional forms of community, workplace leaders need to ensure that realistic expectations are set around what needs the workplace can and cannot meet. This is particularly important as it not only protects the employee from having unrealistic expectations about the role of work in their lives, it also protects the workplace leader or employer from feeling as though they need to meet every aspect of their employee's needs.

This tension was expressed in a number of in-depth interviews we conducted with organisational leaders, including with economist and business leader Ian Harper:

> The advent of social media and the always-on culture creates a set of issues for the workplace that didn't exist when I was starting out. And there's pluses and minuses. In my day, there was such a thing as absenteeism and presenteeism and people would be getting hassled because they felt that they needed to be there by eight o'clock or the boss would notice. And the boss sometimes would do exactly that – they would be in before everybody else and would be the last to leave the office. One of the pleasant aspects of this new technology is that it releases us from the nine to five tyranny.
>
> But there is also a downside. Whereas my generation would feel much more comfortable about saying, 'You don't ring me on the weekend, I work for you from nine to five, Monday to Friday, and on the weekend I don't work for you, so I don't expect you to be in touch with me', now the younger generation would – well, certainly the ambitious ones – would never think twice. Because first, you don't see that demarcation. And second, there's part of you that wants to be contacted. You think, this is quite good, I'm getting contacted, I'm part of this process. So it's become much more difficult to disentangle that.

The upside is that people feel much more engaged as part of the team and the process. And in fact, it's quite exciting. And maybe it is fine that on a Saturday afternoon, two or three people are involved in still working this up. And that's all good. The downside is that people find it much harder to say well, no, enough is enough, and to compartmentalise work.

We discussed how organisations can create an environment for staff to thrive:

It's not wholly altruistic. It is in the end about what makes this organisation a better organisation, but better broadly conceived. I want my staff to be productive. Now they're all knowledge workers who need creativity and stimulus. They need to be able to vacate and take time off to regroup, because creativity tends to wane. People get tired, and possibly bored. So what I need to do is to stimulate you to create an environment in which you take a break in a way that is recreative. And I do that because then, even though you might be working in episodes during the day, the sum total of all of that is much more creative than it otherwise would be.

So the workplace leader is a facilitator, an orchestrator. My job is to create the environment and the framework within which people's purposeful work can enable the organisation to flourish, and them to flourish at the same time.

Work wellbeing needs to be prioritised because people can't have all their needs met through the workplace. A workplace leader should not only ensure their workplace practises prioritise the wellbeing of their teams, but also create environments and work schedules that enable people to have other forms of community and connection outside of the workplace. To summarise the sentiment expressed to us by many young workers regarding work/life balance: 'My work is not my life. It is an important part of my life but not the sum total of my life.'

The concept of work wellbeing is about more than just being tokenistic or implementing tick-a-box workplace practices. Work wellbeing is an attitude embedded deep in the culture of an organisation. It is about how they approach work and valuing their staff as a whole person rather than as just an employee who comes to work. Organisations and their leaders need to be careful that their workplace wellbeing practices aren't purely about increasing the productivity and output of the employees.

Ian Harper gives an insightful corrective to organisations that overplay their important role in supporting their staff:

> What is very destructive is creating the illusion that you can live your life here. I'll provide you with childcare and I'll provide you with wellness, and I'll even feed you. So why go home? You don't need anything outside this. So there's no need for you to belong to a church, pony or golf club any more. This is your family. We are your family.
>
> And this is what happens particularly when community life is eroding, and people are lonely: they will come and they say yeah, this is my workplace. Now I [as the organisational leader] get extra work out of them, because they want to be here. Until of course the time comes, possibly through no fault of theirs, that the business has to change direction. And I say it's been great, but Friday is when you finish up.

This tension for leaders between creating work wellbeing yet ensuring they don't create unhealthy dependency emerged in other interviews with business leaders. Many expressed this tension of shaping environments where people could thrive and authentic community existed without trying to meet all of people's needs.

Daniel Flynn, co-founder of the social enterprise Thankyou, expressed this when he said: 'There is a professional element to work where you're not leading a church, a social community club or a support group. You're leading a business. And in our case you're delivering hardcore commercial outcomes and if you don't you lose, and if you lose you lose everything. It's cut throat. So I think there's a balance within this. I think a part of it is you have to take the pressure off yourself as a leader; you're not everything to everyone.'

Organisations that prioritise employee wellbeing instead of promising that the workplace can fulfil *all* aspects of their wellbeing are key to enabling people to thrive at work. As Daniel Flynn suggests the leader can't be everything to everyone, so not only does this protect and prioritise the wellbeing of employees, it also protects and prioritises the wellbeing of the leader or employer.

While workplace leaders should seek to provide workplaces that enable people to thrive, they also need to support and encourage workers to find a life outside of work and be realistic about what the workplace can offer in the way of life satisfaction and different aspects of a person's holistic wellbeing.

MENTAL HEALTH AND STRESS

It is clear from our worker survey that work can be a key contributor to people feeling stressed and overwhelmed. More than two in five workers (43%) said they always or regularly feel stressed, a third of workers (33%) said they always or often experience work-related stress and 16% said they feel stressed at work to the point that it's a problem. More than one in five (23%) said they always or often experience mental health issues such as anxiety or depression.

Mental health is a pillar of wellbeing. In her book *Thrive*, Arianna Huffington explains that when we look 'at the Western workplace today we see two very different and competing worlds. In one world, we see a clear manifestation of the burnout disorder: a business culture single-mindedly obsessed with quarterly earnings reports, maximising short term profits, and beating growth expectations. In the other world, we see an increasing recognition of the effects workplace stress can have on the wellbeing of employees – and on a company's bottom line.'[2]

When it comes to work, Western culture has elevated being busy to the point of feeling overwhelmed, resulting in a toxic definition of success:

being busy and overwhelmed is something to be proud of. Australians are known for asking and answering their own questions: 'How are you, good?' Or more often these days: 'How is it going: busy?' Indeed, a typical opening to a request is: 'I know you are busy, but …'

Being busy is not necessarily a negative thing. A busy life can be engaging and motivating, and we can feel as though we have a sense of purpose and meaning when we feel like we are contributing. But when busyness and, in particular, workplace stress consistently impede on other significant areas of our life, that's when work can have a negative impact on wellbeing.

To illustrate this concept further, Arianna Huffington uses the powerful analogy of a eulogy to put the toxic definition of success thinking into perspective:

> It is very telling what we don't hear in eulogies. We almost never hear things like: 'The crowning achievement of his life was when he made senior vice president.' Or: 'He increased market share for his company multiple times during his tenure.' Or: 'She never stopped working. She ate lunch at her desk. Every day.' Or: 'He never made it to his kid's Little League games because he always had to go over those figures one more time.' Or: 'While she didn't have any real friends, she had six hundred Facebook friends, and she dealt with every email in her in-box every night.' Or: 'His PowerPoint slides were always meticulously prepared.' Our eulogies are always about the other stuff: what we gave, how we connected, how much we meant to our family and friends, small kindnesses, lifelong passions, and the things that made us laugh.

It's not that work is insignificant amid the other important aspects of life such as family, friends and community contributions. In a recent national study we conducted we asked the question: *If you had your life over again, what would you do differently?* The importance of work was regularly mentioned. Three in five (59%) said that if they had life over again they would have worked harder at their career. More than three in four (77%) stated they wish they had achieved more with their life, and 62% said they would have taken more risks. Some of the biggest regrets expressed were 'not saying yes to more opportunities', 'not making more of my education' and 'not trying harder throughout my life'. While there will be inevitable periods of work-related busyness, this busyness needs to be manageable and enjoyable and interspersed with times of rest to allow workers to refuel and re-energise, so that they can thrive in different aspects of their life.

BURNOUT

Stress and the lack of attention to our mental health are fuelling a workplace condition that impacts millions of people around the world: burnout. According to the World Health Organization:

> Burn-out is included in the 11th Revision of the International Classification of Diseases as an occupational phenomenon. It is not classified as a medical condition. It is described in the chapter as: 'Factors influencing health status or contact with health services' – which includes reasons for which people contact health services but that are not classed as illnesses or health conditions.

> Burn-out is defined as: a syndrome conceptualized as resulting from chronic workplace stress that has not been successfully managed. It is characterized by three dimensions:

- feelings of energy depletion or exhaustion;
- increased mental distance from one's job, or feelings of negativism or cynicism related to one's job; and
- reduced professional efficacy.

Burn-out refers specifically to phenomena in the occupational context and should not be applied to describe experiences in other areas of life.[3]

In our worker survey, 37% said they always or regularly feel busy to the point they struggle to keep on top of things, and more than one in five (22%) said they always or often experience burnout. If sustained over a long period of time, burnout can lead to people resigning and looking elsewhere for a role or organisation that will prioritise their health and wellbeing.

When workers experience burnout they are surviving rather than thriving. It can lead to disengagement and a lack of motivation with the role or organisation if people feel taken advantage of or not appreciated for going over and above. This can in turn lead to absenteeism (taking sick leave) and to presenteeism (where people are physically present while they are unwell, disengaged, distracted or disconnected from what they are doing in the present). When people display presenteeism they are less productive, as their mind is engaged elsewhere. Belgian philosopher Pascal Chabot calls burnout 'civilisation's disease. It's certainly symptomatic of our modern age. It is not only an individual disorder that affects some who are ill-suited to the system, or too committed, or who don't know how to put limits on their professional lives, it is also a disorder that, like a mirror, reflects some excessive values of our society.'[4]

When work takes over life, it can impede on:

* physical health: the need to exercise, sleep and eat well

* mental health: the need to rest, re-energise, be mindful and present and our ability to reduce stress

* social health: the need to connect with others

* relational health: the need to have deep, meaningful connections with family and friends

* spiritual health: the need to find purpose and meaning in life.

Ashley: One of the speakers was a standout at a conference I recently attended on workplace wellbeing. He began with: 'I'm going to say something pretty controversial.' That certainly got everyone's attention. The speaker was law firm head Sam Makhoul, an industry renowned for overworking staff, operating in stressful situations and burnout. Sam delivered a presentation on the importance of sending your staff home on time, of giving people what they really want and need – more time with family. He spoke about how in his organisation people need permission to work beyond 5.00 pm, and that he is advocating the idea of 'the responsible service of workload' (a play on the term 'responsible service of alcohol'). Perhaps the most controversial thing Sam said was that often wellness programs can sound like they are all about worker wellbeing when in fact they are tactics and incentives to make people stay at work longer.

As I thought about this idea more I was reminded of the times I had seen office spaces or workplaces that have lots of amazing features such as gyms, laundry services, shopping facilities and even sleeping pods! While I don't hold a totally sceptical view of the intentions of these workplaces, the fact remains that when workplaces have these sorts of facilities it encourages people to remain at work longer, with the workplace seemingly able to serve any possible need they might have. As Sam himself stated, this idea was quite controversial at a workplace wellbeing conference where lots of speakers spoke about the importance of practical workplace initiatives to prioritise worker wellbeing!

Workplaces that have initiatives around workplace design, ergonomic furniture or other ways of enhancing worker wellbeing must evaluate the key intention behind their practices. Are these initiatives for the wellbeing of the worker or purely for the bottom line of the organisation? Are they to increase the balance and health of the employees or are they purely to increase worker productivity? Healthy and engaged workers will be more productive and high performing, but if that's the motivator rather than the by-product the program will be seen for what it is – a profitability initiative. As Sam Makhoul said, 'Wellness programs won't fix broken cultures.'

While there is a difference between hard work and burnout, workplace leaders need to be on the lookout for their teams and encourage practices that help them to prioritise their workload while allowing time for them to care for and invest in other aspects of their wellbeing. A key difficulty here is that it requires responding to and catering for a variety of different working styles.

In an interview we conducted with Cathy Morcom, a former organisational culture consultant who has worked extensively in both the financial services and not-for-profit sectors, we spoke about the challenge workplace leaders face when trying to encourage workers to maintain a healthy work/life balance and they have a team member who wants to work hard because they thrive through that. The question for the leader becomes: how do you help a variety of different people to thrive without setting an unachievable goal for someone who might have less capacity or who is juggling different priorities in different life stages?

Cathy acknowledged this can be a hard balance to get right and reflected on her own journey. She said: 'That's a really hard question, because I know that one of my strengths and one of my weaknesses is the level of intensity I bring to my entire life. So that is something I constantly need to remind myself about – that people don't necessarily want to, can or wish to work at the same speed.'

When it comes to managing her own working style as a leader and communicating with her team members, Cathy said: 'It will be a conversation I have very early with my team around what their expectations are, what makes them tick, what their communication and management preferences are. I will say to them, "Don't be shocked if I send you an email at ten o'clock at night, because on a Thursday I've got to drop my son to school."'

This transparency and trust between team members is critical to facilitating workplaces where people can work at different speeds and at different times while still being unified towards a common goal. When it comes to avoiding burning people out, creating environments for different people with different working styles to thrive, delivering on organisational metrics and keeping people at the heart of the decisions that companies make are key. As Arianna Huffington put it, 'We think, mistakenly, that success is the result of the amount of time we put in at work, instead of the quality of time we put in.'[5]

THE LONELINESS EPIDEMIC

Workplaces today are facing a loneliness epidemic. Our combined research with Dr Lindsay McMillan shows that almost half (48%) of people in Australia are lonely and that 37% of workers feel lonely at work. In his extensive work on the future of workplaces, Dr McMillan's research paper on workplace loneliness sheds light on the growing epidemic of this phenomenon in the workplace. In the report he said: 'Social connection at work is more than just being happy at work. Humans can easily fake happiness. Instead, it is about contentment and doing good work. The two are not mutually exclusive.'

The report also sheds light on the impact of loneliness on the individual and the workplace. Loneliness can have the same effect on someone's health as smoking 15 cigarettes a day. Not only that, of those who feel lonely at work, 40% felt less productive, 38% reported making more mistakes and 36% reported getting sick more often. Additionally, lonely workers are twice as likely to look for a new job in the next 12 months.[6]

With less distinction between work and home, a decline in people partaking in more traditional forms of community and work subsequently becoming both the second and third space, work is a key contributor to people's sense of community. Workers who are well and whose social needs are enhanced by the workplace are better engaged with their work, thus prioritising work wellbeing for workers is essential to allow thriving people and organisations.

CHAPTER 4

BARRIERS TO WORK WELLBEING

J ust as there is an amazing opportunity for workplaces and leaders to
prioritise the wellbeing of their teams, so too are there barriers that
need to be overcome so that people can thrive and flourish.
In our worker survey we asked: '*In your workplace, which of the following are
blockers to you thriving at work?*' The biggest blocker was being overworked
and stressed (31%), followed by management structures/hierarchy (28%)
and leadership (26%). Seven of these top 10 blockers to thriving are directly
related to leadership, and even the remaining three – general culture, fellow
co-workers and job insecurity – can be significantly shaped by leaders. This
study showed that, in a word, the biggest blocker to workplace flourishing
is *leadership*.

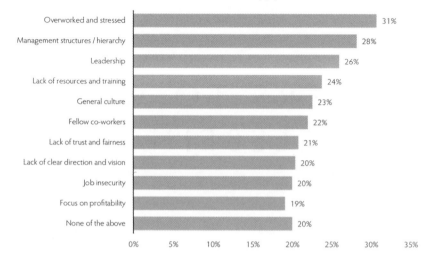

In your workplace, which of the following are blockers to you thriving at work?

Please select all that apply.

Category	Percentage
Overworked and stressed	31%
Management structures / hierarchy	28%
Leadership	26%
Lack of resources and training	24%
General culture	23%
Fellow co-workers	22%
Lack of trust and fairness	21%
Lack of clear direction and vision	20%
Job insecurity	20%
Focus on profitability	19%
None of the above	20%

TOXIC WORKPLACES

If thriving, flourishing workers is the goal and outcome of a healthy workplace, then one of the biggest signs of a negative workplace is toxicity. It can be difficult to define. TopResume says that one way to tell if you work in a toxic workplace is: 'If going to work (or just the thought of going to work) makes you tired, depressed, or even physically ill, that's more than just general work stress; these are the signs of a toxic work environment. A toxic workplace can be defined as any job where the work, the atmosphere, the people, or any combination of those things cause serious disruptions in the rest of your life.'[1]

Employment lawyer and partner Fay Calderone advises organisational leaders and boards on all matters relating to the workplace including discrimination, bullying, harassment, misconduct investigations, performance management, enterprise agreement and industrial disputes. Fay points out that in order for people to thrive and flourish at work, the workplace needs to be psychologically safe. Although higher order drivers of a workplace such as purpose, meaning and mentoring are all significant enablers for people to thrive, we first need to ensure people's basic needs of safety are met. Fay uses Maslow's Hierarchy of Needs (discussed further in Chapter 6) to demonstrate this point:

> In the workplace you need a strong and solid foundation to build upon so people can thrive and flourish. And the most basic aspect of a healthy workplace is that people feel safe, and that the environment is devoid of bullying and other toxic behaviour.
>
> We need to cover the basics of a healthy and psychologically safe workplace culture before organisations can look to mentoring and leadership and personal development, which is at the top of the pyramid.

When we spoke about the indicators of a toxic workplace culture, Fay said that from her experience: 'There's no such thing as trivial behaviour because dysfunction perpetuates. If you don't pick up the little stuff, it inevitably ends up with highly dysfunctional behaviours. The culture of the organisation will be shaped by the worst behaviour the leaders will tolerate.'

In our interview with Melbourne Business School dean Ian Harper, he said that in one organisation he was engaged to lead he became aware of some unhealthy workplace practices. He interviewed every female employee and asked two questions: 'Do you feel safe at this place?' and 'Is this a place where you think you can grow?' Ian related that many women said they felt safe but were not able to grow, which he took very seriously because if half of his staff felt they were unable to grow then obviously the organisation would not flourish.

Ian introduced various methodologies to combat this and to measure and track their progress, including various ways of listening to staff and making sure they were walking the talk of what they wanted to achieve. Ian said: 'None of this is rocket science. It is about trying to make it clear what you're standing for, and then giving people the opportunity to tell you whether you're making this work or not. And to do that in a way that is credible, and that's public. By law my responsibility is to provide a safe workplace.'

PSYCHOPATHS

Another important blocker to work wellbeing and people thriving at work is the presence of a psychopath, or a person lacking empathy. According to David Gillespie, author of the book *Taming Toxic People*, the key traits of a psychopath are that they are: charming, self-obsessed, fluent liars, emotionally manipulative, completely lacking in remorse or guilt, emotionally shallow and callous, have no responsibility for their actions, impulsive, parasitic, fearless, highly controlling, vindictive, aggressive and intimidating.[2] According to forensic psychologist Nathan Brookes, who has studied the traits of corporate leaders, between 3 and 21% display psychopathic traits.[3]

It's not difficult to see how psychopaths can negatively impact a workplace. In a Mamamia podcast, David Gillespie said: 'Workplaces are communities. At the end of the day they are a group of people putting the community or the workplace's benefit or good outcomes above their own. They are doing it for pay so it's not like it is altruism, but it's close. It is putting the benefit of the community above the benefit or outcome of the individual. As soon as people are just there looking out for themselves, defending themselves, and as soon as that's everyone in a workplace doing that, then it means there is a psychopath there.'

LEADERSHIP

There is a popular saying that people don't quit jobs, they quit managers. When it comes to work wellbeing, leaders have a tremendous opportunity to influence the culture of an organisation both positively *and* negatively. In our worker survey, leadership emerged as the third most important contributor to a worker's wellbeing.

More than one in four workers said that management structures or hierarchy (28%) and leadership (26%) are barriers to thriving at work. In another survey we ran in partnership with Reventure we found that 46% of those who planned on looking for a new job believed poor leadership in their workplace was the most stressful part of their job, 42% felt a lot of negative energy in their workplace, 39% said their boss lacked clear vision and direction and 36% were actively looking to leave the organisation because of the leader directly above them.[4]

Employees observe their leaders to decipher what attitude and behaviour is acceptable. Leaders play a huge role in setting the tone, facilitating the culture and communicating and inspiring team members to be their best selves at work.

The Australian business sector watched transfixed for more than a year while the Royal Commission into Misconduct in the Banking, Superannuation and Financial Services Industry held its hearings. The live-streamed hearings showcased efforts to disguise or hide wrong behaviours, along with the scrambling cover-ups and dissembling answers. Reputations were rocked whenever council assisting, Rowena Orr, stated those now famous words: 'Let me show you a document.'

This was the biggest-ever investigation of Australian business, so Commissioner Kenneth Hayne's final report, delivered in early 2019, was greatly anticipated. The overarching theme in the report was that corporate culture was the root cause of the misconduct identified, that culture can both drive misconduct and discourage it. (Culture is further discussed in Chapter 6.)

Leaders set the tone and values from the top but shape the culture from within. Passive leaders create space for destructive cultures to emerge, while controlling leaders produce domineering structures in which behaviours are unchallenged and potential undeveloped.

The authoritarian leadership style is one where a positional leader relies on ranks and roles to dictate policies and procedures within an organisation. They decide what the goals and targets are without any meaningful input from other members of the team. Authoritarian leaders are more like managers who simply tell people what to do, a style that even the military has nuanced for effectiveness. This leadership style leads to a culture of 'us and them' between leaders and employees, broadening the divide and discouraging meaningful participation and worker wellbeing.

For further information refer to Chapter 7.

RETURN ON INVESTMENT

A significant barrier to work wellbeing is a focus on return on investment (ROI). Leaders of organisations do need to focus on outcomes, impacts and financials for their organisation to exist, but if that is the only thing they focus on it can lead to demotivated, uninspired and disengaged workers.

Cathy Morcom talks about the responsibility leaders have to live out the values they profess, and that the KPIs (key performance indicators) and performance metrics they set align with these values:

> If you go to the website of an organisation you will see the mission, which might be about the wellbeing of stakeholders such as customers, employees, regulators, shareholders, society more broadly, and then the values that typically include integrity, excellence, accountability etc. However, that's easier to put on a piece of paper than to actually execute. So a lot of the work I did in organisations was to look at assessment criteria metrics and question: does this demonstrate values-aligned behaviour? Because these metrics manifest to the behaviours.
>
> Some metrics were really questionable because of the incentives that were being offered and because of the short termism around shareholder return. Unfortunately, this focus [on ROI] manifests itself in a move away from the collective and more towards an individual's mindset. And that has an impact on all sorts of things like brand equity, teams, individuals and the organisation. And it also has an impact on the lack of knowledge sharing. If you do have these policies, mechanisms

and systems in place that are going to implicitly or explicitly have you compared against your colleagues, the outcome is that it is going to impact the organisation.

Effective leaders set the tone from the top: they model productivity and wellbeing, and their own example champions the organisational values as they deliver superlative performance. As Cathy Morcom says: 'It's a large responsibility to be a leader in an organisation because people are looking to you for role-modelling behaviours. And if there's an explicit misalignment of behaviour or if there's a misalignment of what people get because of their role in your organisation or how they treat people, it's going to be a major issue with the culture because it's going to be a complete oxymoron.'

Dr Lindsay McMillan reiterated this idea when he said that barriers to work wellbeing exist when 'the task is bigger than the person, that we become so transactional we forget the relational element. That it's all about the performance and it's all about the productivity at the end of the day without the connection to people: at all costs.'

A culture of comparison and competition is incompatible with a cohesive community. The individual members of a team can't compete against each other and be cohesive with each other at the same time. Great leaders build teams that deliver results, and because they prioritise wellbeing their performance is sustainable rather than short term. These leaders aren't driven by fads but by a compelling vision of their future. They don't pivot from agenda to agenda, but rather have a relentless focus on building the capacity of the emerging leaders. They are focused not on the next program but on the next generation.

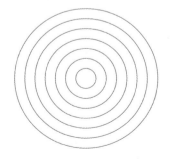

'Returning from work feeling inspired, safe, fulfilled and grateful is a natural human right to which we are all entitled. Not a modern luxury that only a few lucky ones are able to find.'

– SIMON SINEK

TRUST

Another key barrier to work wellbeing is a lack of trust. In order to thrive, workers need to feel trusted by their team and especially by their leaders. Workplaces that have a high level of trust often perform better because workers feel comfortable giving and receiving regular, constructive feedback. When there are high levels of trust people also feel free to make mistakes, which leads to greater innovation and creativity because they know they won't be struck down for having an inferior idea or trying something new that might not work.

High levels of trust are good for both individual and organisational wellbeing. When there is a lack of trust within a team, disengagement and low satisfaction ensue. Employment lawyer and partner Fay Calderone agrees that trust is one of the biggest indicators of a healthy or unhealthy workplace culture:

> There are two ends of the spectrum. People either fear you or they trust you. They are like two pointy ends, so you want trust as the foundation of the relationship with individual team members and trust as the foundation between teams, trusting in each other and trusting they won't throw you under the bus.
>
> So you've got interpersonal relationships as well as the team dynamic, and then feeding into the organisational point of view, trusting that the organisation will do the right thing by the workers – that they will live the values, that leaders will operate with integrity and corporate social responsibility, that they won't do the things we've seen in the media that we don't want organisations to do.

The trust between team members and leadership is very important for fostering both employee and employer/organisational wellbeing. A lack of trust leads to micromanagement, where people don't have the autonomy to undertake their roles.

In team management expert Patrick Lencioni's book *The Five Dysfunctions of a Team*, the first dysfunction is the absence of trust, where the fear of being vulnerable with team members prevents the building of trust within the team. This leads to the second dysfunction, which is a fear of conflict. Conflict can be difficult to cope with; Patrick Lencioni said: 'I don't think anyone ever gets completely used to conflict. If it's not a little uncomfortable, then it's not real. The key is to keep doing it anyway.' He also said 'trust is the foundation of teamwork', and that: 'It's as simple as this. When people don't unload their opinions and don't feel like they've been listened to, they won't really get on board.'[5]

In our worker survey, more than half (55%) said they strongly or somewhat agree they have a high level of trust in those with whom they work. One in five (21%), though, said that a lack of trust and fairness is a blocker to them thriving at work. Leaders have a crucial role to play in facilitating teams that trust each other. According to Patrick Lencioni:

> It is key that leaders demonstrate restraint when their people engage in conflict, and allow resolution to occur naturally, as messy as it can sometimes be. This can be a challenge because many leaders feel that they are somehow failing in their jobs by losing control of their teams during conflict. Finally, as trite as it may sound, a leader's ability to personally model appropriate conflict behaviour is essential. By avoiding conflict when it is necessary and productive – something many executives do – a team leader will encourage this dysfunction to thrive.[6]

When it comes to the practical application of this, Fay Calderone said that trust is about knowing that:

> if you do a good job you will be rewarded and appropriately acknowledged. Trust is if you take flexible work arrangements that you won't lose the opportunity for promotion. Whether it's psychological safety or mentoring or making mistakes or

values or purpose, trust is at the core. A lot of the negative behaviours are about fear and a lot of the positive behaviours are about trust. I would rather empower and entrust my staff 100% of the time and deal with the 1% where they get it wrong.

WELLBEING PROGRAMS

A less obvious barrier to people flourishing and thriving at work can be the façade of wellbeing programs. If people are working in a workplace that has wellbeing practices that lure them to stay at work for longer hours and give more than is expected, this is not conducive to human flourishing and thriving. Organisations that encourage workers to give energy to different spheres of their wellbeing both inside and outside the workplace will help their people to thrive.

If an organisation has the façade of a wellbeing program without it being genuine or helping their employees in some way, or if it is purely about ROI or to cover up negative workplaces practices, it will be a barrier to worker wellbeing.

'Great leaders are focused not on the next program but the next generation.'

– McCRINDLE

CHAPTER 5

PILLARS OF WORK WELLBEING

Martin Seligman identifies three classes of potential positive independent variables when defining positive health. The first is 'subjective assets: optimism, hope, a sense of good health, zest etc'. The second is 'biological assets: the upper range of heart rate variability, hormones, etc'. The third is 'functional assets: excellent marriages, rich friendships, engaging pastimes, and a flourishing work life'.[1]

Personal wellbeing is a key goal people are always striving towards and, as work comprises such a big part of our lives, it is a significant contributor to it. Workplace wellbeing was the top-ranked element in a place of employment, with more than seven in 10 workers (72%) saying it is extremely or very important to them. In terms of importance in a workplace, it ranks above elements such as relationships with peers or colleagues, flexible working hours or workplace leadership.

How people are functioning has a huge impact on the work they do. Conversely, how people function in the workplace has a huge impact on how they function in their everyday life and how they function as a whole. But when it comes to wellbeing at work, whose responsibility is it to ensure that workers are well, and how do the different elements of someone's wellbeing intersect in the workplace?

THE WELLBEING WHEEL

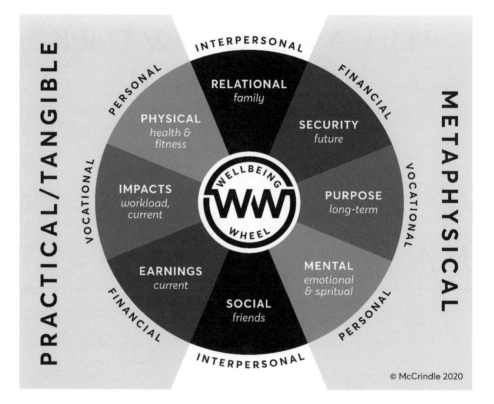

© McCrindle 2020

There are many different approaches that could be used when it comes to wellbeing and the categories we use to define it. In this book we have identified four key components of human wellbeing: personal, interpersonal, vocational and financial.

For three of these four components (personal, vocational and financial) there is a tangible element and a metaphysical element. For personal wellbeing there are physical and mental elements. For vocational wellbeing there are impact and purpose elements, and for financial wellbeing there are earnings and security elements.

Therefore, when it comes to workplace wellbeing initiatives or programs, workplace leaders should consider an holistic approach to the health and wellbeing of their teams.

PERSONAL

Physical health

The physical health of human beings includes physical activity, exercise, healthy eating and nutrition, and one of the most overlooked but most important parts of physical health: sleep.

The shift over the last few decades from an industrial and manual labour economy to a knowledge economy has resulted in increased sedentary lifestyles, greater inactivity and less time spent outside, all of which have negative impacts on people's physical health and wellbeing.

In our worker survey, 64% said that when it comes to their physical health and fitness they felt stressed. Of those, 13% said they felt stressed and it's a problem, while 51% said they felt stressed but it's manageable. A further two in five (40%) always or often don't get enough exercise, with 13% saying they *always* fail to get enough exercise.

When we spend too long at work, feel too stressed by our workloads or don't have enough energy because of work, it has a flow-on effect on other areas of our life. One in two workers (49%) said they struggle to make physical health and fitness a priority, that it is the first aspect of life to suffer because of work.

The second physical aspect that suffers because of work stress is sleep, with two in five workers (41%) saying they struggle to make sleep a priority. Sleep is essential for cognitive function, creativity and overall health and wellbeing, and two in five workers (39%) said they always or often don't get enough sleep. Furthermore, only 34% of workers are extremely or very satisfied with their sleep patterns, which is among the lowest ranked areas of life in terms of satisfaction.

Matthew Walker, author of *Why We Sleep*, said: 'Sleep is the single most effective thing we can do to reset our brain and body health each day.' He also said: 'When sleep is abundant, minds flourish. When it is deficient, they don't.'[2] In her book *Thrive*, Arianna Huffington says: 'Sleep deprivation reduces our emotional intelligence, self-regard, assertiveness, sense of independence, empathy toward others, the quality of our interpersonal relationships, positive thinking, and impulse control.'[3]

While the level of physical health and fitness is largely the individual's responsibility, workplaces can play an important role in helping their staff be physically well. It often begins with workplace design, where ergonomic furniture, standing desks and fruit bowls all exist to ensure physical health in a workplace is being looked after.

Workplaces that have a culture of working overtime negatively contribute to people's physical health and wellbeing. The longer you work the less physical activity you partake in, the less time you spend with your family, the later you eat dinner and go to bed and the poorer quality of sleep you get. Workplaces that encourage people to leave on time and have regular breaks from sedentary work and prioritise healthy eating and physical activity practices will contribute to their workers' ability to thrive physically and therefore vocationally.

Emotional and spiritual health

The World Health Organization (WHO) defines mental health as a state of wellbeing in which every individual realises his or her own potential, can cope with the normal stresses of life, can work productively and fruitfully and is able to make a contribution to her or his community. The positive dimension of mental health is stressed in WHO's definition of health as contained in its constitution: 'Health is a state of complete physical, mental and social wellbeing and not merely the absence of disease or infirmity.'[4]

More than two in five workers (43%) always or often feel stressed in life. Additionally, 37% always or regularly feel busy to the point they struggle to keep on top of things. When it comes to the causes of this stress, four in five (79%) say their work is a cause of stress. Of those, 16% say work causes them stress and it's a problem, while 63% say work causes them stress but it's manageable.

In our survey, we asked workers how often they experienced various elements of stress. The survey found that 37% of workers always or often feel rushed or pressed for time, 33% experience work-related stress, 33% experience frustration, 23% experience mental health (anxiety or depression) and 22% have experienced burnout.

In *Flourish*, Martin Seligman identified that: 'Positive mental health is a presence: the presence of positive emotion, the presence of engagement, the presence of meaning, the presence of good relationships, and the presence of accomplishment. Being in a state of mental health is not merely being disorder free; rather it is the presence of flourishing.'[5]

Positive emotions play a crucial role in personal flourishing. This includes both a positive mindset (experiencing gratitude, optimistic thinking, positive mindfulness) and positive emotions (fun and enjoyment, satisfaction, safety and pride). Positivity is linked to longevity, broadens thinking leading to more creativity and improved decision making, builds resilience and has an 'undoing' effect on negativity. The workplace can have a significant impact on emotional wellbeing by ensuring that workers are encouraged and supported, have an opportunity to reflect and find balance in their lives, find enjoyment in their work and that the workplace is a healthy environment.

> **Ashley:** A member of my team had some personal challenges outside of work. I spoke to them about these things and was surprised to hear that during this challenging season, work was a safe place for them. Because there was so much uncertainty and stress outside of work, work became a really positive place, an escape from the stress of other demands. This taught me that the workplace can have a really positive impact on people personally if the workplace and leaders in it facilitate environments where people feel safe, valued and accepted.

Another component of personal wellbeing that relates to human flourishing and thriving is spiritual wellbeing, which concerns feeling that your life has a lasting meaning and is connected to a higher purpose. Martin Seligman said: 'There is considerable evidence that a higher level of spirituality goes hand in hand with greater wellbeing, less mental illness, less substance abuse, and more stable marriages.' He goes on to say: 'It [spiritual fitness] supports and encourages the search for truth, self-knowledge, right action, and purpose in life: living by a code that is rooted in belonging to and serving something [people] believe is larger than the self.'[6]

The most recent Census results in Australia showed a decline in the proportion of the population engaging with traditional religions, with a significant drop in the proportion of the population identifying their religion as Christianity (from 61% to 52%) and a rise in those identifying with no religion (from 22% to 30%).

Our faith and belief report expanded on this and quantified those who, while not identifying with a religion, still identified as spiritual. Our research found that 45% of Australians identified with Christianity, 9% identified with all other religions, 32% did not identify with a religion and 14% identified themselves as being spiritual but not religious. Those who are spiritual but not religious are most likely to believe there is an ultimate purpose and meaning in life (36%). One in four of them (26%) believed in the inward journey of discovering the inner person. One in five (22%) believed in a mixture of spiritual beliefs from major religions.

While spirituality is a deeply personal journey, workplaces can still take into consideration this aspect of their workers' wellbeing and how spirituality contributes to a sense of meaning, purpose and personal wellbeing.

INTERPERSONAL

Social health

Human beings are social creatures. Four hundred years ago, John Donne summarised the futility of self-sufficiency and the importance of community with his words 'No man is an island'; an intrinsic human need we all have is belonging and acceptance. In *Your Wellbeing Blueprint*, Michelle McQuaid and Penny Kern write:

> A sense of belonging correlates with a range of positive outcomes, including higher self-esteem, greater life satisfaction, faster recovery from disease, lower levels of stress, less mental illness, and a longer life. Loneliness, social isolation, and the lack of social support place a person at high risk for psychological distress, physical and mental illness, and early mortality. This is why research suggests that more than what you're doing at work, it's who you're doing it with that ultimately determines your levels of engagement and wellbeing. For example, if you have a best friend at work, you're seven times more likely to be engaged in your job, produce higher quality work, and have higher levels of wellbeing.[7]

In our worker survey, one third (34%) said they struggled to make friendships a priority, and just 31% said they felt extremely or very satisfied with how connected they were in the community.

With a third of the hours in an average week spent at work, the nature of work changing and a shift in how we spend our time outside of work (more time on screens, less time in face-to-face interaction), the workplace plays an important role in the social needs of human beings. To some work is simply a job, but to many more it's a lifeline to social interaction, purpose and a place of belonging. Therefore, twenty-first-century workplaces are not just where workers come to work; they are for many the primary environment in which people find community.

Workplaces are also facing a loneliness epidemic, with loneliness defined as being disconnected from others and viewing your relationships negatively. More than a third of workers (37%) feel lonely at work, and almost half (48%) sometimes feel lonely outside of work.[8] Work contributes to people's social needs which, increasingly, people are not getting from more traditional sources such as places of worship, sporting clubs and even their families. Work is becoming a new aspect of community. The Workplace Loneliness report from A Future that Works states: 'The human experience seems to be lost in Australian workplaces. Workers expect workplaces to provide social connectedness, but this expectation has not been met. Decision makers in our organisations need to appreciate that their workplaces can and should provide opportunities for social interaction to help reduce loneliness in the workplace.'[9]

Workers have spoken. In our survey, 72% of workers said wellbeing is the most important part of a workplace, and 83% said workplace wellbeing was extremely or very important and that it is the responsibility of the employer. Furthermore, three in four Australian workers (74%) agreed that a leader at work is responsible for whether someone in the team feels lonely.

How do leaders create environments and opportunities for cohesion and connection? The Workplace Loneliness report suggests that workplaces:

* raise awareness
* prioritise wellbeing in wellbeing programs
* prioritise social connectedness from the start
* focus on values
* create and foster a culture that encourages kindness and compassion
* incorporate solutions that cater for all age groups
* include employees in designing solutions
* increase opportunities for social interaction during work
* celebrate team members' achievements in person
* foster a collaborative learning culture
* include remote workers
* identify 'champions' for social connectedness.[10]

The best leaders facilitate purposeful community; social needs are met, but in a collegiate setting. These teams are not just social networks: they are missional tribes that are diverse but have a passionate purpose. Great leaders bring unity to the diversity; for them, diversity is an asset, not a symbol, and they enhance it with an emphatic answer to the question 'Inclusive to what?'

It is also important to remember that people bring their home to work, just as they bring their work home. As Plato said: 'Be kind, for everyone you meet is fighting a hard battle.' When workplaces connect with people and allow them to be who they are in whatever season they are in, and we rehumanise work and remember that we are leading emotional and social people, not robots or machines, it will serve to help our workplace communities and create environments where people can thrive.

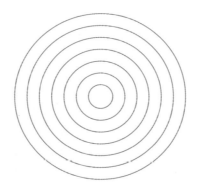

'Great leaders
bring unity to the
diversity; for them,
diversity is an asset,
not a symbol.'

– McCRINDLE

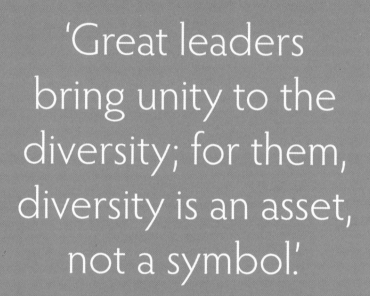

Relational health

Like the social element, the relational element is another part of the interpersonal sector of the wellbeing wheel. 'Relational' refers to our familial relationships and is the area in which workers feel the most satisfied, with 55% of workers saying they feel extremely or very satisfied with this area of their life. However, a third of workers (34%) have struggled to make friendships a priority, while more than a quarter of workers (27%) say they have struggled to make their family a priority.

In the realm of positive psychology, of which Martin Seligman is a key contributor, the elements of wellbeing include positive emotion, engagement, meaning, accomplishments and positive relationships. In reference to the latter element, Seligman says in *Flourish*: 'When asked what, in two words or fewer, positive psychology is about, Christopher Peterson, one of its founders replied "other people".' Seligman goes on to say: 'Very little that is positive is solitary. When was the last time you laughed uproariously? The last time you felt indescribable joy? The last time you sensed profound meaning and purpose? The last time you felt enormously proud of an accomplishment? Even without knowing the particulars of these high points in your life, I know their form: all of them took place around other people. Other people are the best antidote to the downs of life and the single most reliable up.'[11]

While this pillar of wellbeing refers to relationships outside of work, it is one of the most significant to the individual. Dr Lindsay McMillan, author of many reports about workplace wellbeing and one-time leader of Converge International (one of the most experienced corporate mental health-care providers in Australia), said Converge conducted about 300,000 hours of counselling. We asked what the four issues that get in the way of performance and productivity were:

> The first big one that gets in the way of performance and productivity is relationship breakdown at home. What does that say? It says that work is now not defined by nine to five. You bring home stuff to work and your work stuff home. The

second is stress, anxiety and depression. The third is toxic workplaces: I'm treated badly by my boss. The fourth is grief and loss: what happens if I'm going to lose my job, and all the implications of that?

While workplaces can't be the solution in all circumstances, they can help to support people going through personal circumstances, particularly those pertaining to relational breakdowns and grief and loss.

Workplace leaders will do well to view people in their context, acknowledging that behind an individual worker is a life of other interests and relationships. Opportunities for people to talk about these aspects of their life, share with colleagues, go home on time or be viewed as more than just an employee are key to enabling people to thrive. Co-founder of Thankyou Daniel Flynn writes in *Chapter One*:

> For me, the assumption that your team is a wider group than just your direct staff was an obvious concept, so I was caught off guard at our staff Christmas party a few years back. I had just gone around the room and individually thanked every person while sharing stories about each of our team, and then I thanked the wider team (spouses and partners) for their support. Afterwards, several of our staff's partners came up and commended me for thanking them. Many of them said they had never felt so valued ever for being a 'partner', and very few said they had even considered themselves as part of our team. Perhaps because Jarryd, Justine and I all work with our spouses, we realise the impact having complete support from your spouse or your partner has. It's incredible![12]

Recognising that people who work for you or with you are more than just the person in front of you, that they are part of other personal relationships and important personal commitments is key. When people feel supported as a whole person at work rather than as just an employee who comes in to do a set of tasks, it creates a significant opportunity for them to thrive. It's time to think holistically about the workplace, beyond just business outputs.

VOCATIONAL

The word vocation means a strong calling or inclination towards a particular career or profession. Martin Seligman defines vocation as 'being called to act rather than choosing to act – it is an old word, but it is a real thing'. He goes on to say: 'Sociologists distinguish among a job, a career, and a calling. You do a job for the money, and when the money stops, you stop working. A calling, in contrast, is done for its own sake. You would do it anyway, with no pay and no promotions. "Try to stop me!" is what your heart cries when you are thwarted.'[13]

For some, talk of finding a career that aligns with their passion and sense of mission may sound overly zealous. Yet we are finding that even among the most clear-eyed of the next generation, values alignment and a commitment to the organisational cause are prerequisites for a job search. In an era of an ageing workforce and where there are more jobs than people young people are empowered in the recruitment equation, which is why it has been called the war for talent. No longer is it simply a fair day's work for a fair day's pay. As we say to our clients: 'People aren't working for you. They may be employed by you, but they are working for their own reasons. Think of them as professional volunteers.'

Impacts

The impacts of our work are key to a sense of vocation. As humans we want to know that our work each day is contributing to something bigger, that we are making a difference. Measuring organisational impacts and sharing these with the team you work with is foundational to employee motivation. Employee satisfaction is directly linked to the impacts people see they are having and from the work they are doing. A fulfilling workday means getting to the end of it and saying: 'It was a good day. I really felt like I shaped or contributed to something.' To stand up from a desk or walk off a job knowing that what you did that day made a measurable difference, helped someone or shaped an outcome enhances wellbeing.

Purpose

While impact refers to the current workload, purpose takes an overarching look at the reasons behind why we work. Having a sense that our work fulfils us and that what we do is part of a higher calling provides the meaning we derive from work. Great leaders not only know why their organisation exists but how to best communicate this to their staff. Wellbeing is enhanced when employees feel they have a purpose behind why they do what they do.

A strong sense of purpose is also important for motivating and inspiring workers. Through different seasons and circumstances we all need to be motivated and inspired, and a clearly articulated organisational purpose can do that. Purpose can unite and encourage people to get out of bed, come to work and deliver the impacts. Work is about more than financial reward and immediate deliverables; it plays a huge role in our sense of contribution, value, purpose and meaning.

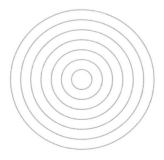

'People aren't working for you. They may be employed by you, but they are working for their own reasons. Think of them as professional volunteers.'

– McCRINDLE

FINANCIAL

While the workplace is not responsible for workers' personal finances, it certainly contributes to them and therefore to worker's wellbeing. Almost three in four workers (74%) said they felt stressed when it came to their personal finances. Close to one in five (18%) said their personal finances caused them stress and it was a problem, while 56% said their personal finances caused them stress but it was manageable. Just under one third of workers (31%) said they were extremely or very satisfied with their financial situation, which is among the lower end of the spectrum when it comes to satisfaction in different areas of life such as relationships, sleep patterns and personal fulfilment.

During the shutdowns associated with COVID-19 it became very clear early on to governments worldwide that the financial impacts would cause many greater problems than the virus itself. Aware of the lack of personal savings and the financial vulnerability of workers, the Australian government implemented its JobKeeper program, which was the biggest spend on any social program in Australian history. Our research at the time showed that 49% of Australians said they were extremely or very emotionally resilient (mental health), 40% were extremely or very physically resilient (overall health) but only 30% felt extremely or very resilient financially.

Earnings

For most people the main contributor to financial wellbeing is earnings via salary or wages. Therefore, job security is an important factor for wellbeing. Our survey of workers revealed that one in five workers (19%) always or often experienced job insecurity.

Due to the precarious nature of the current job market, with the gig economy and part-time or casual work options more readily available than ever before, job insecurity is having an impact on employee wellbeing. While contingent work (part-time, casual or project-based work) provides flexibility with hours and pay, this flexibility can also be a cause of concern.

Security

Along with the social, relational and vocational elements, the stability and security of having a job or working situation where people feel they are somewhat stable or secure in the future is important for worker wellbeing. In our study on precarious workplaces for Reventure we found that, while Australian workers are moving jobs more frequently than in the past, 96% said job security was considered to be extremely or very important to them. This same study also found that more than seven in 10 (72%) expected it will be harder (definitely/somewhat) to find jobs in the future.[14]

When Generation X first entered the workforce, just one in 10 employees were not full time. Now, as Generation Z move into their working years, this proportion has tripled to more than three in 10. There are many factors behind this, but it is still the case that helping people to feel financially secure in their role provides a key component of employee wellbeing.

WHOSE RESPONSIBILITY IS EMPLOYEE WELLBEING?

In our worker survey we asked the question: '*When thinking about mental health issues in Australia today, work-related stress and workplace-related conflict, to what extent do you think employers have a responsibility to ensure wellbeing among their staff?*' More than four in five workers (83%) said that it was extremely or very important and that it is the responsibility of the employer. Specifically, 46% said it was extremely important and that wellbeing, like workplace safety, is essential for employers to ensure. A similar proportion, 37%, said mental health, work-related stress and workplace-related conflict were very important and should be prioritised.

The view that wellbeing is extremely or very important and is the responsibility of the employer is even more prevalent among the emerging generations. More than four in five Generation Zs (85%) and close to nine in 10 Generation Ys (87%) think wellbeing is extremely or very important and is the responsibility of employers.

Only 13% of workers said wellbeing was somewhat important and that it should be a combined approach: that the employer along with the staff member has a responsibility to manage this. Just 4% of workers said wellbeing was slightly or not at all important and was the responsibility of the employee to manage.

Workers expect employers to be responsible for their teams working well, yet it shouldn't be denied that the responsibility also lies with the individual. In the many interviews we conducted with leaders from the not-for-profit sector through to the corporate sphere, this key insight emerged about wellbeing and employee fulfilment: while employers and workplace leaders have a role to play in facilitating environments where workers can thrive, it is not solely their responsibility.

Many leaders related how they tried so hard to fulfil all aspects of their teams' wellbeing that it burnt them out. While we hope leaders take the wellbeing of their teams seriously, leaders need to understand their responsibilities and the limits of their role. Leaders need to know when to recommend that employees seek support beyond the workplace. While the workplace cannot meet all of a worker's needs, it plays an important role in creating the enabling conditions and environments for people to flourish.

'To some work is simply a job, but to many more it's a lifeline to social interaction, purpose and a place of belonging.'

– McCRINDLE

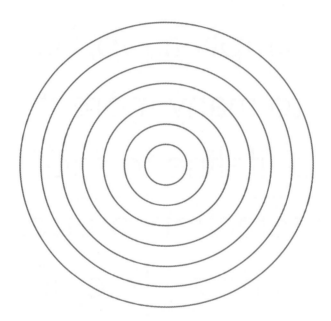

CHAPTER 6

HOW TO FOSTER WORK WELLBEING

With the gig economy in full swing and the emerging generations changing jobs more frequently than ever before, it is harder to attract and retain staff. This is particularly true for the emerging generations. Generation Z, who have grown up and been shaped by vastly different conditions than any other generation, seek leadership opportunities and don't need a job purely for survival and security reasons. What is important to this generation of emerging workers is the community they seek in their workplace, a clear vision to which they can contribute and celebration of the hard work they are putting into their roles. In summary, employees are looking for what we call the *CPI engagement equation*, where employment engagement = culture + purpose + impact.

© McCrindle 2020

CULTURE

In a workplace, culture is the environment that, whether intentionally or unintentionally, is created for workers. Simon Sinek said: 'Culture = values × behaviour. A culture is strong when people work with each other, for each other. A culture is weak when people work against each other for themselves.'[1] He also said:

> A company is a culture. A group of people brought together around a common set of values and beliefs. It's not products or services that bind a company together. It's not size and might that make a company strong, it's the culture – the strong sense of beliefs and values that everyone, from the CEO to the receptionist, all share. So the logic follows, the goal is not to hire people who simply have a skill set you need, the goal is to hire people who believe what you believe.[2]

If we think about different elements of a workplace, *competence* is about what an organisation does and the fruit it produces or the outcomes of employees' work. *Cause* is why an organisation exists, its purpose. *Culture* is how an organisation does things, the root level that impacts other aspects of the organisation. If a workplace has a negative or unhealthy culture it can flow out into other aspects of the organisation, including interaction with clients and customers.

COMPETENCE
what we do

CAUSE
why we exist

CULTURE
how we do it

© McCrindle 2020

Culture is the character and personality of your organisation, what makes your business unique, and is the sum of its values, traditions, beliefs, interactions, behaviours and attitudes. Positive workplace cultures attract talent, drive engagement, impact happiness and satisfaction and affect performance. The personality of your business is influenced by everything, including leadership, management, workplace practices, policies and people.[3]

We wanted to test how important culture and values alignment is, so in our worker survey we pitted it against other important factors in the workforce to see which, on the whole, workers valued more. We asked the question: *'When looking for a place of employment, which matters most to you: the organisational culture and values alignment or the conditions, earnings and salary package?'* Amazingly, for more than half of all workers (58%) organisational culture and values mattered more than remuneration! While workplace culture is important for all workers regardless of age, it is key to attraction and retention for the emerging generations.

The workplace facilitates a need that we have as human beings: connection and belonging. Previous generations likely had their social needs met through connection points outside work, such as local service clubs, community organisations and places of worship. They were less likely to rent, moved less frequently and had more regular connections with their neighbours. The emerging generations, however, look for community and connection in their workplace because they are more geographically mobile and are spending more time in digital communities rather than through face-to-face interactions. The timeless human need for social connection is unchanged, however, the social connection points have changed. The emerging generations are looking to the workplace for social needs and connection along with professional collegiality and development.

Transactional and transformational workplace cultures

Culture can be quite complex to understand and difficult to communicate. It involves various aspects from why an organisation exists to how things are done, high-level thinking and practical outworkings, and aspirational values and rituals or behaviours. When it comes to an organisation's focus, it can be easy to develop a 'transactional' culture that focuses on survival aspects such as profit margins, stakeholders and shareholders. These aspects of an organisation are important, but if we want to lead thriving teams then developing a transformational culture is key.

TRANSACTIONAL CULTURE	THE BIG SIX	TRANSFORMATIONAL CULTURE
Value	Why?	Authentic values
Output	What?	Positive impacts
Clients	Who?	Flourishing community
Workplace	Where?	Relevant context
Management	How?	Enlarging leadership
Immediate	When?	Thriving legacy

Engaging workplace cultures have as their *Why?* not the transactional focus on value alone, but the transformational driver of their authentic values. Similarly, the *What?* of an organisation's existence is not output, but positive impacts. The focal point of their attention, the *Who?*, is not clients alone – as important as they are – but the communities that they serve including staff, suppliers and the opportunity to create flourishing communities at large.

Transformational cultures define their *Where?* not just by the physical aspects of the workplace, such as the office or job site, but by the era and context in which they operate. *How?* they operate depends not on management structures, but on leadership that enlarges the capacity and longevity of their organisation.

Finally, transformational cultures consider not only the short-term perspective of their work; their *When?* is focused on long-term impacts and leaving a thriving legacy.

Consider an iceberg: the transactional column is the top of the iceberg, what can be seen above the water. The value, output, clients, workplace, management and short term are all important and visible parts of an organisation's culture and priorities, but below the waterline is the transformational culture. It is deeper and larger, driving and impacting what is above the surface. When organisations focus on the transformational culture it will contribute to their teams' and their own ability to thrive.

Mark: During the challenges presented by COVID-19 our organisation, like so many globally, was forced into the terrible situation of having to make some of the roles of our team members redundant. How the decisions are made around letting someone go reveals whether an organisation has a transactional or transformational culture. When I shared with my team leaders the realities of our context and the bitter consequences of what it would mean for two of our valued colleagues, the occasion overwhelmed me. Like many of my generation I'm not much of a crier, but I know I wasn't alone in getting emotional in those dark days. Like all of us leaders who try to develop a transformational culture, our staff are not employees but team members with whom we are, together, building something significant. When the leadership mantel requires us to make decisions such as this, necessary though they may be, they make for the darkest days. Peter Drucker, the father of modern management theory, was well known for his efficiency measures, performance strategies and goal frameworks. Despite his commitment to management strategies, he was famous for saying: 'Culture eats strategy for breakfast.'

Dr Jen George, founder and director of social enterprise Comcorp, which promotes positive social and environmental change, said:

> You can understand purpose at many levels, including at the individual level. To earn an income is purpose. However, to believe in the purpose of an organisation is another thing altogether, and that is the key difference between a transactional job and being in a job that creates a community that is engaged in a shared purpose.
>
> When people who work together find their shared passion and turn that into an organisational purpose then they can find community, because they find a connection deeper than just being about themselves. That's where it becomes transformational. We are wired for community. And where you find people connecting at a community level, wellbeing increases.

PURPOSE

Purpose refers to the 'why' of an organisation, the big picture of what the organisation is about: their reason for existence. Organisations need to know why they exist as the starting point upon which to build a strong team culture.

When we asked workers what matters more – purpose and vision within an organisation or job security and longer tenure – almost half (46%) said purpose and vision were more important than job security and tenure when considering a place of employment.

In his book *Start with Why*, Simon Sinek said: 'Very few people or companies can clearly articulate why they do what they do. When I say why, I don't mean to make money – that's a result. By why I mean what is your purpose, cause or belief? Why does your company exist? Why do you get out of bed every morning? And why should anyone care?'[4]

Meaning and purpose are key contributors to wellbeing and a sense of fulfilment. Martin Seligman says in *Flourish*: 'Human beings want meaning and purpose in life. The Meaningful Life consists in belonging to and serving something that you believe is bigger than the self.'[5] It is essential organisations have a strong sense of purpose for their teams to align to. More than half of workers (55%) say that a strong mission, vision and values are extremely or very important to them in their place of employment. When organisations have a purpose and it is clearly communicated it provides an opportunity for people to align to and be motivated by that purpose. When we have purpose in our personal and work lives it enables us to thrive and flourish.

In our worker survey, 57% strongly or somewhat agreed that they find purpose and meaning in their work. Similarly, 54% strongly or somewhat agree that what they do for work is making a difference in people's lives. While these are positive findings, it also indicates that just under half of workers *do not* find purpose and meaning in their work or feel as though what they do for work is making a difference in people's lives. When asked whether efforts are made to help people find purpose and meaning in their work, one in two workers (50%) strongly or somewhat agreed. Clearly, there is work to be done in our organisations to ensure that more people find purpose and fulfilment in their work.

In his book *The Culture Code*, Daniel Coyle talks extensively about the importance of having a purpose and how to build it. He says that building purpose 'is not as simple as carving a mission statement in granite or encouraging everyone to recite a hymnal of catchphrases. It's a never-ending process of trying, failing, reflecting and above all learning. High-purpose environments don't descend on groups from on high; they are dug out of the ground, over and over, as a group navigates its problems together and evolves to meet the challenges of a fast-changing world.'[6]

It's not just any purpose such as making more money for shareholders that motivates, gives meaning and enables workers to flourish. Organisations with purpose that is transformational and impactful are ones that will attract customers, inspire loyalty and build community. The saying 'It's not personal, it's business' shows a misunderstanding of both the purpose of business and the broad realm of the personal. Business at its best delights customers, rewards team members and positively impacts broader society.

Having a clear purpose also helps to attract the right people who believe in it and want to work for that purpose for an organisation. Purpose inspires; it helps to retain. Simon Sinek said: 'Great companies don't hire skilled people and motivate them, they hire already motivated people and inspire them. Unless you give motivated people something to believe in, something bigger than their job to work toward, they will motivate themselves to find a new job and you'll be stuck with whoever's left.'[7]

Positively, 88% of workers know the vision and mission of the organisation they work in, and 87% agree with this vision and mission. When a community is aligned to the same purpose, it facilitates environments where people trust each other more. We trust those with whom we share common values or beliefs, and trust is essential for thriving teams. A sense of purpose that aligns with that of others in the community or organisation helps to strengthen our sense of belonging; it can change our entire view of our job and make us more productive, innovative and loyal. When workers embody the cause or purpose of an organisation they become brand ambassadors, giving better service to customers and clients and communicating the purpose to their family, friends, clients, customers and community.

The Net Promoter Score (NPS) is a customer engagement tool that measures the willingness of customers to recommend a company's products or services to others. It is used as a proxy for gauging the customer's overall satisfaction with a company's product or service and the customer's loyalty to the brand. Customers are asked: *On a scale of 0 to 10, how likely are you to recommend this company's product or service to a friend or colleague?'* Based on their rating, customers are then classified into three categories: detractors (those who give a rating of 0-6), passives (those who give a rating of 7-8) and promoters (those who give a rating of 9-10).[8] The NPS formula involves subtracting the detractors (0-6) from the promoters (9 and 10). A score above 0 (more promoters than detractors) is desirable.

We developed a new index to measure the willingness of employees to recommend a company as a place to work and called it the Net Culture Score (NCS). We asked the question: *'On a scale from 0-10, how likely is it that you would recommend your organisation as a place to work, where relevant, to a friend or contact?*' As with the Net Promoter Score, those who selected a 9 or 10 were considered to be the organisation's promoters, speaking to others about it very positively. As expounded in Chapter 7, organisations that have a clear and compelling purpose and empowering and enlarging leaders consistently have more engaged employees as measured by the NCS.

People go out of their way to recommend an organisation with which they engage on a visceral level. Even more powerful than the 'raving fans' as measured by the NPS are the passionate staff members as measured by the NCS, because they promote both the product brand and the employer brand. In our worker survey, 57% strongly or somewhat agreed that they are motivated to work hard because their job is interesting and important to them personally.

Patrick Lencioni said in *The 5 Dysfunctions of a Team*: 'Engaged, enthusiastic, and loyal employees are pivotal drivers of growth and health in any organisation.'[9]

As Simon Sinek points out, having a strong sense of purpose motivates workers through stressful circumstances: 'Working hard for something we don't care about is called stress. Working hard for something we love is called passion.'[10]

When people embody a sense of purpose it inspires those around them and connects on a personal level. Purpose also provides an anchor point for people during busy seasons. Simon Sinek said:

> If the people inside a company are told to come to work and just do their job, that's all they will do. If they are constantly reminded why the company was founded and told to always look for ways to bring that cause to life while performing their job, however, then they will do more than their job . . . If you hire people just because they can do a job, they'll work for your money. But if you hire people who believe what you believe, they'll work for you with blood and sweat and tears.[11]

When integrity results from an organisation's purpose being delivered, trust is built and loyalty is earned. These are the by-products of a strong purpose or vision (why you exist) and a concise mission (how you go about achieving that vision) and will ensure a positive culture. However, something that works well for one organisation won't necessarily work well for another. Why? Because each organisation has a unique story and will articulate their purpose and raison d'être differently.

An organisation's purpose and having a sense of why it exists should act as a filter for all decisions to ensure they align with the values of the organisation. Having a strong purpose can live on through generations and contribute to an organisation's legacy, so it's important to keep revisiting the purpose. In *Start with Why* Simon Sinek said: 'All organizations start with WHY, but only the great ones keep their WHY clear year after year.'[12]

Generation Z and Maslow's Hierarchy of Needs

Developed by Abraham Maslow in 1943 during World War II, the Hierarchy of Needs is a pyramid-shaped, five-tier model of human needs. The basic human needs of survival (physiological) and security (safety) comprise the largest tiers at the bottom, with higher-order needs such as social (love and belonging), self-esteem and self-actualisation at the top. The theory is that the most basic human needs of food, water, warmth, rest, security and safety need to be met before humans can or are motivated to move on to psychological needs such as love and belonging. At the top end of the model are the self-fulfilment needs of self-esteem and self-actualisation; these needs are about achieving your full potential. 'The original hierarchy states that a lower level must be completely satisfied and fulfilled before moving onto a higher pursuit. However, today scholars prefer to think of these levels as continuously overlapping each other.'[13]

In the context of work, *survival and security* needs are components such as remuneration, employment conditions, superannuation, worker entitlements, role description, tenure and job security. The *social* needs include opportunities for collaboration, social events, co-working spaces and team building. The *self-actualisation* needs are things such as the triple bottom line (people, profit, planet), organisational values, corporate giving programs, career pathways, further study, training and personal development.

The same principles of Maslow's hierarchy can be applied to the workplace: when survival and security needs are met (when staff are paid fairly and have stable job security) they will seek out the higher-order drivers that lead to greater self-fulfilment and wellbeing. In our generational analysis we observed that the emerging generations in particular are searching for these higher-order drivers in their places of work. In fact, many in the next generation arrive at their career life stage with the bottom two tiers already fulfilled. They therefore start their organisational search at the social level and make their decisions based on tiers four and five as well. This higher-order focus is true not only for attraction, but also for retention. It is not the presence of push factors from their organisation that drives voluntary turnover, but the absence of pull factors back towards the employer. In other words, many young people leave jobs not because there is a compelling reason to leave but because there is no compelling reason to stay.

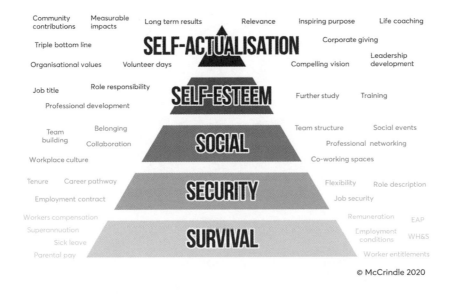

© McCrindle 2020

The findings are clear: organisations that know why they exist and are able to effectively communicate their purpose will not only attract workers who will align to their purpose, it is also likely they will retain them for longer.

'Many young people leave jobs not because there is a compelling reason to leave but because there is no compelling reason to stay.'

– McCRINDLE

IMPACT

'A team that is not focused on results stagnates/fails to grow, rarely defeats competitors and loses achievement-oriented employees.' – Patrick Lencioni

The third part of the engagement equation is impact. A transformational culture is about more than just the outputs; it is about the impact an organisation and the team members are able to have. When an organisation is able to measure their impact other than just by the outputs in numbers or KPIs it can lead to greater engagement and input from team members.

Impact refers to the contribution team members can make to achieve the purpose an organisation has. It's no longer just enough to provide the fortnightly pay as their thank you; workers want to know that their contribution is making a difference.

Impacts are highlighted by celebrating wins and celebrating people, and sometimes by awards and non-monetary rewards. It is both an opportunity for employees to contribute and a celebration of the impact those individuals or the team are having. Whether the impacts are on a large or small scale, sharing and celebrating the impacts an organisation is having are important.

For more than two in five Australian workers (43%), the impact an organisation is able to have is more important to them than the employment conditions and entitlements.

We identified three actions to help organisations focus on the impact they are having: contribute, challenge and celebrate.

Contribute

A key part of our ability to thrive is to have meaning, or 'belonging to and serving something that you believe is bigger than the self'.[14] Workers are motivated when they feel like their work has meaning, and that through it they are contributing to the overall purpose of the organisation and to something bigger than the organisation. Contributing to the greater good beyond daily work practices can be facilitated through volunteer days, corporate giving programs or by simple steps to support a cause.

In his extensive work on human flourishing, Martin Seligman identified that achievement and growth are two key aspects of getting the most out of life and contribute to thriving. When workers feel they are achieving something, when they contribute to discussions or the work being done, they are more likely to be satisfied in their work and in their life. When workers are part of a productive group, they feel the esprit de corps – the spirit of the team.

Challenge

In order to have an impact, workers need to feel challenged in their role, because challenges lead to growth and growth is essential for wellbeing. Benjamin Franklin said: 'Without continual growth and progress, such words as improvement, achievement, and success have no meaning.' As any personal trainer will advise, muscles are strengthened through resistance. From lifting weights to pushing against the resistance in a spin class to fighting gravity in a squat, without challenge there is no growth.

Celebrate

The third C to focus on, and perhaps the most tangible and overlooked, is the need to celebrate the contributions of the team and the challenges people overcome. Celebrating how a team moves together to achieve the organisation's purpose and the impact they have is crucial to engagement. It can range from thank yous to awards, rewards or providing social time. In our worker survey, only one in two workers (50%) strongly or somewhat agreed that their managers and leaders offered feedback, rewards and recognition. This indicated to us there is plenty of room for leaders to improve on how they celebrate their teams.

Regardless of the sport or the level of skill, sporting teams continually celebrate good plays with high fives, back slaps and encouraging feedback. When a goal is scored or a victory won, the celebrations are loud and infectious. Context-appropriate celebrations are an important rhythm of any team in any setting.

Celebrating fulfils a deep human need, creates connection between people and a sense of belonging, is an inexpensive investment, yields return in terms of productivity and contributes to team morale, employee engagement and workers' wellbeing.

> **Ashley:** We have a team composed largely of those in their twenties and thirties, so we have a mix of Generation Z and Generation Y in our workplace. As a team leader I know the importance of focusing strongly on celebrating the wins and highlighting the impacts. We begin our weekly meetings by dedicating time to sharing with the rest of the team some of the wins. We deliver positive client feedback to the team and celebrate the big and small wins together. We have found that these positive words really build each other up and encourage one another. We show the output of what people have been working on and celebrate people for their achievements.

The need to celebrate people, impacts and wins is demonstrated by Thankyou co-founder Daniel Flynn:

> In 2008 I led a group of university students in the establishment of a social enterprise called Thankyou Water. Our aim was to launch a bottled water product that would exist for the sole purpose of funding water projects in developing nations.
>
> It was a tough start-up journey and we encountered a lot of setbacks along the way. We were a group of young people with limited business experience, but we had loads of determination

and that was what drove us to continue building the business even through the tough times.

In July 2013, after already having secured major deals with 7-Eleven Australia and Australia Post for our bottled water, we rebranded to Thankyou and launched two new ranges: Thankyou Food and Thankyou Body Care. The reason behind this was to enable us to fund food, health and hygiene projects in developing nations as well as water projects. We also launched a bold campaign that resulted in Coles and Woolworths agreeing to stock our entire range of products, which catapulted our business into a season of strong growth and meant our impact through our projects grew exponentially. Our aim is to keep growing so we can continue to impact many more lives in need, because we believe that together we can help end global poverty.

Aside from the amazing impacts Thankyou is having on people around the world, the organisation has also experienced rapid growth. Flynn reflected on Thankyou's journey and the importance of celebrating the wins as a team, saying if he could wind back the clock he 'would be enjoying the process, celebrating the wins along the way'. He admitted that in the early years worries over issues in the business and his relentless drive to push things forward probably had a negative effect on some of his team: 'We landed 7-Eleven, which was a huge deal, and that was in year three. Instead of celebrating that, I said: "We've really got to focus." I think in entrepreneurism and in business ownership, the great strength of that business mind is to keep on wanting the next thing and moving forward. The mistake is you burn out the people around you. Ideas won't be fostered when you suck all the life out of the room.'

A business mentor helped Flynn realise he was not celebrating the small wins along the way with his staff, or even alone. Now Thankyou has regular catch-ups, such as a fortnightly team news time to share their wins and recognise staff who have performed well: 'If we have a really big win as a team we'll stop and celebrate. It could be just pizzas or whatever it is.'[15]

Team successes without celebrations provide a fast track to burnout, but a community of workers who contribute together and overcome challenges and celebrate the wins is a compelling force. The best teams are diverse in age, gender and culture but are united in purpose, values and ambition. Like any community, therefore, they are defined by their centre, not their circumference. An enlarging leader strengthens the diversity by bringing inclusion through a compelling vision. For more on enlarging leadership see Chapter 7.

Remember our CPI formula for what employees are looking for in an organisation. If an organisation has a great inclusive culture and a very clear, visionary purpose but there is no impact or celebration of wins, then it is not motivating. Similarly, if an organisation has a compelling purpose and the team have excellent impacts as they move towards this purpose but the culture is divisive and anti-social, then clearly it won't engage staff. All three elements are required to create an engaging and inspiring organisation that workers want to be a part of.

'The best teams are diverse in age, gender and culture but are united in purpose, values and ambition . . . they are defined by their centre, not their circumference. An enlarging leader strengthens the diversity by bringing inclusion through a compelling vision.'

– MCCRINDLE

CHAPTER 7

LEADING TEAMS IN CHANGING TIMES

I n an effort to describe the extent of change we've experienced, the previous decade introduced new terms such as 'disruption', 'megatrends' and 'change fatigue', and the unprecedented use of the word 'unprecedented'. We live in a digital economy, our device playlists are generated by artificial intelligence, online stores use predictive algorithms to make purchasing suggestions and primary school students are learning coding and robotics.

As we entered the 2020s we surveyed Australians to get a measure on how they were feeling about the amount of change they experienced in the last decade. The biggest response was 'concerned', the feeling of more than one in three respondents. This was much larger than the one in four who were feeling 'positive', and for every person feeling 'empowered' almost twice as many were feeling 'overwhelmed'. Similarly, far more felt 'fatigued' than 'energised'. While many motivated leaders find it an exciting time to be alive, many in our organisations are more subdued.

Amid global influences, a volatile economy, emerging (and declining) jobs and accelerating technological change, many workers are feeling uncertain. The stark reality was pointed out by Justin Trudeau in his speech at the

World Economic Forum: 'The pace of change has never been this fast, yet it will never be this slow again.'

An understanding of the trends can give a better vision of where we're headed, and an observation of the emerging generations can give some foresight to prepare us for what's next. Today's university students have never known a world of printed encyclopaedias, phone books, street directories, video rental stores or fax machines. Most in the next generation along – Generation Alpha, born since 2010 – will never use a desktop computer, analogue watch, physical credit card or car ignition key. In a world of electronic driver's licences and e-payments, most will never own a wallet. By observing these shifts we can gain an understanding of the trends and be ready to respond to the changes.

Leaders need to be responsive to the changing cultures, generations, backgrounds and expectations that comprise their teams. They've got to spend more time listening and understanding, not just speaking and directing. In his book *The 7 Habits of Highly Effective People* Stephen Covey said: 'Seek first to understand then to be understood.'[1]

This is the core business of the leader. The key characteristic of a leader is foresight: the reason they can lead is that they know the way to go. Leaders see things not just as they are, but as they will be. They not only observe the changing times; they understand them. They don't just get impacted by the trends; they proactively respond to them. They not only adapt their own direction based on the shifting landscape; importantly, they lead others on the journey. The future will always be to some extent uncertain but, like a good surfer who keeps an eye on the horizon, leaders maintain situational awareness and are prepared for the changing seas and ready to surf the waves.

'The pace of change has never been this fast, yet it will never be this slow again.'

–JUSTIN TRUDEAU,
WORLD ECONOMIC FORUM

WELLBEING AT WORK STARTS WITH LEADERSHIP

Leaders play a crucial role in the development of an organisation's culture. Gallup stated in their Approach to Culture report: 'Culture is the organisation's GPS, giving its employees routes and pathways for living the organisation's purpose and delivering on its brand promise. But unlike a typical GPS system, culture is not always obvious. It is communicated regularly by what leaders say but even more importantly by what leaders do and the decisions they make.'[2] Workplace leaders set the mood and tone of work environments, making or breaking the development of a culture of wellbeing. Employees look to leaders for what behaviour, customs, attitudes and ways of communicating are favourable and acceptable.

So how can leaders create environments where their staff can thrive personally and professionally? By creating a culture of leadership growth, personal improvement and team development – in short, by being an enlarging leader.

WE NEED LEADERS, NOT BOSSES

The word 'boss' was used in previous generations to denote a leader, although it carries negative connotations of ordering and commanding, of 'bossing' people around. Workplace leadership should never be authoritarian or garner results through intimidation or aggression. Google search is a useful research tool to find out, through the prompted search suggestions, what the most searched phrases are. We typed 'bosses are' into the Google search bar and the top three search phrases were that bosses are:

❖ bullies

❖ sociopaths

❖ psychopaths

Clearly many people's experiences of bosses have been poor. As a popular sign says: 'Don't just stand there doing nothing. People will think you're a boss!'

> **Ashley:** Teachers in a focus group were discussing what makes a positive staff culture. One of the participants said: 'You can tell by the language people use, whether they use "them" or "we".' Everyone in the group agreed. It became apparent to me that this insight was true and reflective of the 'boss' language. When people use the word 'boss' to describe their leader or manager, it does seem there is a separation of that boss from the team whether or not it's intentional. The boss isn't one of us, the boss tells people what to do, which is not what a 'leader' does. A leader brings people alongside them, and leads from within the team and for the team, not for themselves.

LEADERSHIP STYLES

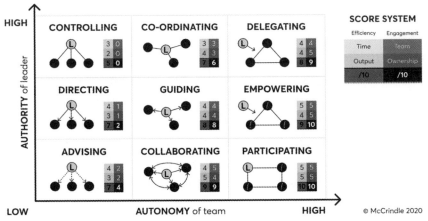

© McCrindle 2020

The leadership spectrum chart displays the array of leadership styles based on the level of authority used by the leader (from low intensity to highly authoritarian) and also the autonomy of the team (from low independence to high ownership). The scoring system rates four aspects of efficiency and effectiveness, each out of five, for a possible maximum score of 20.

Under the efficiency category are time effectiveness (a measure of the efficiency of each person's application to the task) and output effectiveness (the total output achieved by the team). While autocratic leadership such as controlling or directing styles have been thought to offer good efficiency, they will inevitably lose out on team engagement measures. However, our observations of such teams is that when the fear of failure is high or uncertainty is great, as exacerbated by an authoritarian leader, time efficiency wanes as team members double guess their approach. This paralysis by analysis factor also impacts on the output efficiency. Leaders are not involved in the task and don't overly support the process, so the total output is impaired.

As the indicative scores show and as allocated from our observations, efficiency is actually heightened as the authority exercised by the leader eases. The team members step up to leadership functions, the leaders themselves are involved in the process (which further contributes to the effectiveness of the team) and the capacity of the team members grows and their output increases through their task involvement. Additionally, as the autonomy of the team increases, decisions are made in situ rather than requiring approval or decision making from a leader who is separate from the context, which again increases the efficiency scores.

The other two measures sit under the engagement category: team engagement in the process and team ownership of the results. It is self-evident that when the leader is more authoritarian in style the team is less engaged in the process; after all, it is the leader's program. Additionally, a high-authority leader will result in less team ownership of the task as they are just doing what they have been told to do. The engagement metrics of the teams with a leader as controller, director or co-ordinator are well below those of the leader as participator, empowerer or collaborator.

Analysis of the leadership spectrum shows that the participating style gained the top score of 20, followed by empowering (19), with collaborating (18) and delegating (17) not far behind. In descending order from these we have guiding (16), coordinating (13) and advising (11), with the lowest scores going to directing (9) and controlling (5).

The lines and locations of the leader and team indicate the direction of the interaction. Some are top down (hierarchical), while others are more grouped (participative). Some lines are connected (control), while others have arrow heads indicating input and support rather than command. Some arrows point one way (chain of command), while others flow both ways (interaction). Some lines are dotted, indicating opportunity for input rather than a definite reporting line. And while each model has an official leader, marked by an 'L', other models also have developing, functional leaders who will no doubt emerge to be team leaders (marked by an 'l').

Clearly, the leader will adapt their style based on the experience of the team, the complexity of the objective and the current priority of the organisation (as it shifts between task urgency and team development). There may be times when a controlling or directing style is required but high authority/low autonomy is not the place for a leader to live. While leadership styles will be situation dependent, it is our contention that leaders who are participating, empowering and collaborating will not only result in more efficient outcomes and more engaged teams, but they will also foster a culture of wellbeing in their organisations. In these approaches the leader leads by example from within the team and the team collaborates to deliver outcomes. Additionally, these leadership styles characterise people who not only show their team how to lead by leading with integrity, but who also consciously look for opportunities to develop other leaders. This is what we have called 'enlarging leadership', as the results are greater team capacity, enhanced performance and developed leaders.

The last few decades have seen a clear move away from the command and control leadership styles towards the collaborative leadership style, which was confirmed in our worker survey when we asked the question: '*Thinking about the following leadership styles, what is your preference and experience?*'

The most common leadership style people experienced when they first began their career was the authoritarian style (31%), followed closely by the hierarchical leadership style (30%).

When we asked about what sort of leadership style people currently experience, the most common style was the co-ordinated style (35%), followed by the hierarchical style (27%) and the collaborative style (24%). Just 14% of workers said they currently experience an authoritarian leadership style.

Finally, we asked workers what leadership style they prefer. The majority of workers (40%) preferred a collaborative leadership style, closely followed by 38% who preferred a co-ordinated style. Just 16% preferred a hierarchical leadership style, and 6% preferred an authoritarian style.

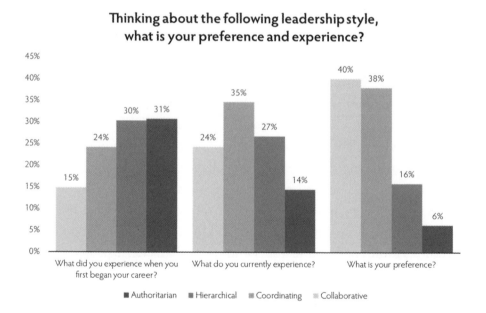

Thinking about the following leadership style, what is your preference and experience?

Workers have spoken: they want to be employed in workplaces and organisations in which leaders are collaborative and coordinating rather than hierarchical or authoritarian.

We also wanted to find if leadership styles and priorities correlate to a return on investment in the workplace, so we looked at the different transformational factors of leadership (collaborative style, people focused and long-term perspective). We tested these against their impact on employment outcomes (staff advocacy, employee engagement and staff retention):

* To determine a worker's advocacy we asked: 'On a scale from 0-10, how likely is it that you would recommend your organisation as a place of work to a friend or contact?' This question gave us a Net Culture Score (a score from -100 to 100).

* To determine a worker's engagement we asked: 'Thinking about how engaged you are in your current role, on a scale from 0-10 please rate your current engagement with your workplace and role.' This question gives us a Net Engagement Score (a score from -100 to 100).

* To determine a worker's retention we asked: 'If it were up to you, on a scale from 0-10 how likely is it that you will still be working at your current place of employment in two years' time?' This question gives us a Net Retention Score (a score from -100 to 100).

We have compared results across two styles of leadership: collaborative and authoritarian.

Workers who experienced a collaborative leadership style in their workplace were 3.6 times more likely to be advocates of the organisation. The Net Culture Score of those who experienced collaborative leadership was 14.95, compared with those who experienced an authoritarian style having a Net Culture Score of −38.69.

Similarly, those who experienced a collaborative leadership style at work were more likely to be engaged at work. The Net Engagement Score of those who experienced this leadership style was 19.57, 2.5 times more than that of those who experienced an authoritarian leadership style, having a score of −29.17.

Those who experienced collaborative leadership styles were 2.7 times more likely to stay in their current place of employment. Those who experienced this style had a Net Retention Score of 17.08, compared with those who experienced authoritarian leadership styles having a score of −29.17.

Leaders who lead with authenticity and create a culture of collaboration will enable a thriving workplace. When leaders are responsive and collaborative and focus on the wellbeing of their teams, they will not only lead the interactive Generation Zeds effectively but also future generations.

LEADERSHIP PRIORITY

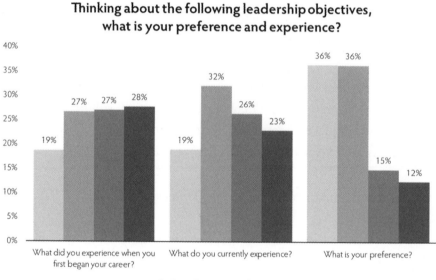

Thinking about the following leadership objectives, what is your preference and experience?

With regard to leadership priority, we identified the four key priorities a leader focuses on: profit (monetary focus), output (product/productivity focus), goals (KPIs and objectives) and people (prioritising and valuing the team).

When they first began their career, the majority of workers experienced a focus on profit (28%), followed closely by output (27%), goals (27%) and people (19%). When we asked what they currently experience, the majority of workers experienced a focus on goals (32%), followed by output (26%), profit (23%) and people (19%).

When it comes to leadership priority, workers' preference is for it to be on the people of the organisation (36%) and the goals (36%) more so than on the output (15%) or the profit (12%).

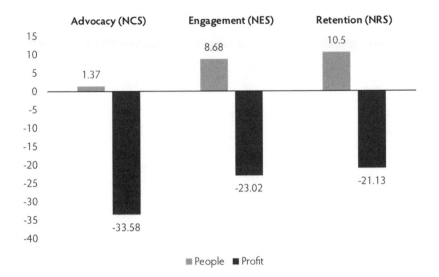

When leaders focus on people over profit, workers are much more likely to be advocates of the organisation, have better engagement and stay longer with the organisation. The Net Culture Score of those who experienced leaders whose focus was on people was 1.37, compared to −33.58, meaning they are far more likely to be advocates for the organisation. Those who experienced a leadership priority of people also had a higher net engagement score (8.68) than those whose focus was on profit (−23.02), and they also had a higher Net Retention Score of 10.5 than those who experienced leaders with a focus on profit (−21.13).

The people-focused leader produced positive measures in each category compared to the extremely negative staff advocacy, engagement and retention results of the profit-focused leader. This study clearly shows that the leader who prioritises the wellbeing and development of their team members will be rewarded with brand advocates, engaged employees and lower turnover.

'The success of a
leader is measured
not by what they
achieve in their life,
but by what they
set in motion.'

– McCRINDLE

LEADERSHIP PERSPECTIVE

Thinking about the timeframes a leader uses to measure how well the organisation is achieving its purpose, what is your preference and experience?

When it comes to perspective, a leader can have either a predominantly short-term, medium-term, long-term or legacy perspective.

In our worker survey, medium-term (36%) and short-term (35%) leadership perspectives were the most common when people first began their careers, with medium term (41%) and long term (29%) the most commonly experienced in workplaces today. When asked about their leadership preference, the majority of workers prefer medium term (39%) and long term (36%), with around one in 10 (11%) preferring a legacy leadership perspective, which is double the proportion who had experienced it at the time of the survey (5%).

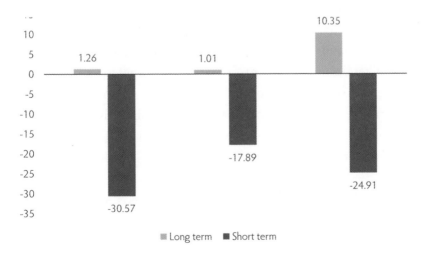

We grouped the leadership priorities into two groups, long term (incorporating long term and legacy) and short term. Not only do workers prefer a long-term approach in the workplace, this leadership perspective correlates to higher advocacy, engagement and retention among workers than a short-term perspective does. Consistent with each of the previously discussed leadership aspects, the perspective a leader brings comprehensively shapes the staff engagement achieved. Leaders whose perspective is long term have positively advocating staff, engaged teams and better retention compared with those who have a short-term focus, in which case the resulting outcomes are all negative.

Clearly, workers respond better to collaborative and co-ordinated leadership than they do to authoritative and hierarchical leadership. Leadership style expectation has shifted away from traditional models to an engaging one.

Leadership priority has also shifted. While the management theory might focus on systems, structures and processes, workers want the leadership priority to be on the people. Workers are looking for organisations that prioritise people through training and growth and ensure they are functioning at their best.

Our study also showed the positive outcomes when leadership perspectives shift from a short-term focus, such as monthly, quarterly, or even annual results, to longer term considerations such as the enhancement of the team. Those who focus on growing people and their skills are best placed to be able to shape team culture. Leaders who bring a collaborative style over a command and control style will have a better chance of attracting and retaining top talent. To attract competent and efficient staff, help them thrive in the workplace and retain them, organisations need to champion the best leadership style (collaborative), leadership priority (people) and leadership perspective (long term). The success of a leader is measured not by what they achieve in their life but by what they set in motion.

One leader who has demonstrated these different aspects is Andrew Scipione, former commissioner of the New South Wales Police Force. During his tenure

Andrew was widely acknowledged as positively transforming the culture of the force. We asked Andrew about his career in the police force, which had a negative culture, and about some of the challenges and complexities of leading over 16,000 police officers (one of the largest police forces in Australia). When Andrew shared thoughts about his leadership style, priorities and perspective, it became clear he prioritised people, had a long-term focus and led with authority without it being about power and control:

> First and foremost, decisions that come from the top communicate what is accepted and what is not accepted within an organisation. I learned that the destiny of the organisation is shaped by its people, and that my job as the commissioner was to impact the generation of police I had at the time when I was in charge, as well as those to come and the police force going forward. I saw things happen that should not be happening as a police officer.
>
> I realised that if we didn't start dealing with this culture, this culture would tear us apart. So that had to come from my time, from me. I had to sack a lot of police. And often it wasn't for what they did, it was because of what they covered up.
>
> I swore in 8,000 police in my time as commissioner. I stood not only in front of them but in front of their friends and families, and I said to every single one of them: 'If you lose my confidence, you will lose your job.' With cultural change, if you're in a position of crisis like we were, you can't afford to have a slow transition; it would have been like creeping death. We couldn't have said that we've got a 10-year plan to change, it had to be almost catastrophic change.
>
> As the commissioner of an organisation or a CEO, if you have the courage you can turn it around, because courage is infectious just like fear can be. If you go to a situation where there is a little bit of fear running through a community, that can run like wildfire. In the same way, if you can start to bring

courage to the front line, it grows. It grows confidence, it grows capability, it grows commitment and it grows courage. You see, policing is not really a career, it's a calling. You can't give a person enough money to have them turn up every day for 40 years and put their life on the line.

We said to everyone that had already given so much that this is the direction we're about to go. And make no mistake, if you are going to join us then we're going to do everything we can to look after you, because you matter and you count. But if you don't see yourself fitting then now is the time to get off the train, because once it leaves there's no going back. And it's got to be that stark. It has to be that clear. And that can be tough. You need to be courageous. That's what leadership is about.

Making tough decisions is the calling and responsibility of a leader and, while difficult, the best leaders make these tough calls because they know in the long term they will help the people they serve – from those inside the organisation to the clients, customers and communities they operate in.

This concept came through in an interview with Tim Sims, founder of Pacific Equity Partners, an Australasian private equity investment firm that focuses on leveraged buyout and growth. Tim has vast experience advising chief executives and large corporations on how to grow profits and value. He spoke about the human challenges of business such as redundancies and said that dealing with such challenges is always difficult:

Until a leader has carried the overhead cost of less competent employees, they often don't want to deal with the issue. Until they have seen the dysfunction and the poor quality, the sense of injustice to more junior people, until they have experienced the bitterness of that, it is very hard to ask a person to depart your organisation. Asking a person to leave a job and doing it personally is always hard, but it is particularly hard if you don't know what the implications are of not addressing that issue. And they can be catastrophic for organisations. They can completely undermine the clarity and purpose of organisations and they can even destroy organisations. Without that pruning and necessary ventilation of organisations, mediocrity or excess cost isn't addressed. It is always hard and miserable. But experience tells you it has to absolutely be addressed.

Sadly, these are the darker responsibilities of leadership. From experience, seeing as it is such an unpleasant thing to do it needs to be done quickly, in a timely way, and it needs to be done generously. When the decision is delayed it makes it harder to be generous; it undermines or damages people who are struggling in roles inappropriate for them. A timely response, clear explanation and generous behaviours are fundamentally necessary in conveying bad news. It is never fun, but not doing it has a far greater cost for the organisation and people involved than doing it. People in business a long time know that and tend to be willing to do that even though it is difficult.

Leaders need to make difficult calls if they are committed to prioritising their people and are focused on the long-term perspective of the organisation.

Andrew Scipione said that while he often had to make difficult and hard decisions it was in the service of his community, and people appreciated his strength in doing so. He also says that his leadership style, while strong and firm, was not authoritarian or command and control because first that is ineffective and second it must never be about the leader:

Leadership is all about influence. If you go through and think about the leadership decisions you've had to make, often it's about influencing people or the organisation or the future. That doesn't mean that you don't stand with authority and exercise that authority responsibly. It's all about what you say, how you say it and what you do. That's influence. That's true leadership.

I had to make sure that I exercised leadership understanding, that I was more about trying to build people up and help them to deliver their potential, to take them to the point where they were able to perform well above what they thought they could in order to get the maximum return back to those they served. But that didn't mean you didn't do the hard stuff. I had more threats from cops that I had sacked than from criminals – and I had a lot of threats from criminals. You're taking away their very livelihood, but you need to be strong in the organisation and people need to know that is the way it is. We've never needed stronger leaders in our history than we do today. We need them in every sphere of life.

The leadership style someone uses to influence those they are leading contributes to the wellbeing and ability of people to thrive in their environment. Andrew Scipione's leadership style held authority, focused on the common good of the community and those he was leading and had a long-term perspective. In a hierarchical industry, he brought authority without being overpowering or domineering, which produced a deep respect among the community and his officers during his tenure and service.

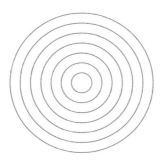

'The key characteristic of a leader is foresight. The reason they can lead is that they know the way to go. Leaders see things not just as they now are, but as they will be. They not only observe the changing times; they understand them. They don't just get impacted by the trends; they proactively respond to them. They not only adapt their own direction based on the shifting landscape; importantly, they lead others on the journey.'

– McCRINDLE

CARING LEADERS

We have no doubt that organisational leaders have many competing priorities to juggle. Profit margins keep businesses and organisations alive and absolutely need to be given appropriate time and consideration. However, if our research has shown us anything, it's that successful organisations prioritise the people they lead and care about them as more than just employees.

We asked Tim Sims how leaders can best help their teams to thrive:

> [As leaders] we need to be highly motivated by balance. We need to work hard but understand when rest is necessary. We need to be kind but understand when firmness is necessary. We need to be driven by the numbers but understand that sometimes there is something beyond the numbers that can create momentum, which you can't see in an accounting profile.
>
> Most of all, we need to realise that the way the person in the organisation relates to another person is disproportionally modelled on how the leader or chief executive behaves. When I was running small organisations, if I came to the office for no good reason with a long face or looking a bit down, literally I could see through the glass walls that the mood of the office was different. And so modelling a degree of controlled optimism is important.
>
> A great businessman I once worked for managed a vast supermarket chain. He was immensely wealthy and incredibly gifted, but what he modelled was a deep sense of concern for every ordinary person in the organisation. He frequently used to say the smartest customer in the world is the housewife. The most important person in the business is my employee. And he demonstrated this when he went on store visits or was in the office. He would say: 'How are you', 'How is trading today?', 'How are you feeling?', 'How is your family?' He showed a genuine interest, not a passing superficial interest but a genuine interest in the wellbeing of his people and modelled that for others.

Different businesses differ, but the focus will always be: what are we purposed to do here? What behaviours will optimise that on a sustainable basis, and how do I model that as a leader?

Leaders play a critical role in developing and creating environments where people care about each other and feel cared for, which allows people to respect and trust one another, give feedback, challenge each other and innovate together. Daniel Coyle sums this up well in *The Culture Code*: 'One misconception about highly successful cultures is that they are happy, light-hearted places. This is mostly not the case. They are energized and engaged, but at their core their members are oriented less around achieving happiness than around solving hard problems together. This task involves many moments of high-candour feedback, uncomfortable truth-telling, when they confront the gap between where the group is, and where it ought to be.'[3]

Another leader we interviewed for his perspective on work wellbeing was George Savvides. George has had three CEO assignments across 24 years including 14 years as CEO of Medibank, and has been chairman of Next Science Ltd, deputy chair of the Special Broadcasting Service (SBS) and director of IAG and Ryman Healthcare.

In our interview we discussed leadership and the importance of it in successful companies. George spoke about leaders who overcame seemingly insurmountable obstacles and developed great teams that lead high-performing organisations with amazing results. He said that organisations with high-performance teams do better than their competition; have the energy and discretionary effort to tackle unsolved problems, use innovation to solve them; and become more relevant as a result of improving themselves. They are able to do these things because of a leader who is not concerned with self-interest, popularity and personal success but who resists the gravitational pull of selfishness, pulls away from the drug of authority and demonstrates care for their teams and their people:

The role of transformational leadership, purpose and high-performing teams is often deprioritised well below financial engineering, strategy and M&A [mergers and acquisitions]. Yet the power for high performance exists within the organisation and its leaders. They just need to know how to unlock it.

Organisational transformation is powered by leadership and employee engagement centred on a clear sense of purpose and customer needs. Leaders who empower employees like coaches invite employees to put their talent forward to solve complex organisational problems and care for the nurture of the team.

Transformational leaders know leadership is not about them, it's about the assignment they have been given to steward. They know it's not about being a leader with all the answers or the one who scores all the goals. They know the talent is in the team and the leader's role, like a conductor, is to unlock that talent and let it be expressed. Such leaders shepherd the team through the frequent distractions of individual self-interest and friction with colleagues and shift the focus on to the mission and its impact on clients, beneficiaries, the community and beyond.

Leadership is about the mission, not ambition, and a convicting purpose is what attracts the heart and convictions of employees because they want to make that why happen. When leaders invest in unlocking the talent and the team, by caring for that team, engaging with the team, validating talent across the table, calling in and practising as a team, working to solve problems that haven't been solved, people go to work feeling validated.

It's through kindness that you get power that delivers effort. It's not through force. In the corporate world, we have to know our leader's best interest really is in the care of the team.

George told a story about his time at Medibank:

One of the project leaders had just gotten back a prognosis around breast cancer. She had taken time off from work to get treatment, so the team was very keen to look after her. [I told HR] 'Please provide whatever the company can do in terms of base care. The company will just be generous and look after her.'

What I didn't expect was the reaction, that it magnified the care message from above, that this organisation really cares. And it created a kindness, that this is a team that cares. We became more aware of circumstances around employees in times of struggle, and we became more responsive to their needs. I learned a lot from that: that leaders [need to be] people leaders and not just corporate leaders.

When workplaces are communities and people feel they are cared for beyond just getting the work done it creates environments for people to trust each other more and produce better work.

George used the analogy of a rowing race to illustrate the idea of leaders who lead from within their teams and produce team connectedness, which in turn produces high performance in organisational culture and effort that innovates: 'In rowing competitions one type of power leader shouts at people, pumping his heart as hard as he can. Then another boat glides past them, because that team is totally connected on heart, passion and conviction: the leader is within them. The good news is that the data says the leader who invests in the team produces the high-performing, long-term and sustainable organisational outcomes.'

THE LEADER AS EMPOWERER, ENLARGER AND COACH

Researcher and author Jim Collins, in his best-selling book *Good to Great*,[4] discusses his concept of the 'level 5 leader'. His research confirmed that long-term high performance in organisations is linked not to the tangible advantages (such as unique technology and scarce raw materials) but rather to the DNA of the leaders in them. He says level 5 leaders are more like coaches being characteristically humble and caring deeply about their organisational outcomes.

Archetypal leaders are like captains who dominate the limelight, often score the winning goals, have rank, are highly visible on the field and are directly associated with success. However, Jim argues that more effective are level 5 leaders: they are less visible, working behind the scenes, preparing and counselling the team, creating alignment and laying the groundwork for long-term success. In short, they believe the talent is in the team and encourage good behaviour and reprimand negative behaviour in service of the bigger goal and organisational purpose. One of the key attributes of such leaders is that they put the team and the team's needs above themselves.

George Savvides said that when he was asked to step out of his non-executive board role at Medibank into an acting CEO role for a few months following an unplanned exit of the previous CEO, he was not experienced in health insurance:

> The assignment was to provide stability to the organisation while the board commenced a CEO search process. A few weeks later it became apparent that the health fund had lurched into record losses and was under close surveillance by the prudential regulator. I met with the regulator several times to understand the seriousness of the situation: we had a burning platform.
>
> I travelled to Canberra to brief the health minister, seeking her support for the measures that needed to be addressed and implemented. We were in trouble. The largest health fund in the country was perilously close to defaulting on member claims. We had no money for consultants. I was an unqualified leader who could not read the insurance hymn sheet or speak the 'technical' language, and I had 3,000 frightened employees angry toward management for having made the company a public embarrassment and placing their jobs and livelihoods at risk. This was the assignment I was asked to step up to.
>
> My leadership instinct, learned from previous CEO assignments, was to go to our employees and tap into the relationship power of the team (the talent is in the team)

and invite their creative contributions to solve the company's problems. By travelling around the country, I met all the staff with their supervisors and we established a teamwork plan and with the urgency that came from our burning platform. We had no problem defining our purpose and mission: it was survival, regaining dignity and not letting our four million customers down. I did not have the answers, but I didn't need to. My role was to empower our staff to work together, invite the teams across the whole organisation to contribute the hundreds of solutions that, when implemented, shifted the broken organisation back to health and to a 'good' company once again. Within a couple of years the $175 million loss was turned back to a modest profit.

But we had more to do if customer relevance and customer needs were to be met. The second half of the 14-year CEO journey was to move the organisation from good to great, not because of a management whim but because of what our front-line staff were sharing from our customers. In its broken state in 2003, Medibank was valued at $800 million, or close to net tangible assets. When it was restored to good company performance in 2007 it was independently valued at $1.8 billion when a possible privatisation was being considered. Following its purpose-led transformation into a healthy company, I had the privilege to lead the IPO onto the ASX in 2014, where it was valued at $5.3 billion. When I retired in 2016 after 14 years as CEO it was valued at $6 billion, and today it's valued at $7 billion.

We had the privilege of interviewing John Anderson, former deputy prime minister of Australia and leader of the National Party from 1999 to 2005. Another empowering leader, John was acting prime minister on 11 September 2001 when reports came through of the terrorist attacks in the United States. He described this as being one of those darks days when leaders have to ask themselves some hard questions:

Are you serving yourself, or are you genuinely serving others and prepared to make whatever sacrifices are necessary, putting your own self-interest aside? And that is really the ultimate test of leadership: are you prepared to lay down your life for others? I remember actively praying at the time. What happened to me was inconsequential in terms of my responsibility to the Australian people. The advice was that there might very well be a series of attacks and anything could happen, anywhere, including Australia, and I had a very deep sense that the buck was stopping with me. It was a very profound moment for me. I found comfort in having been able to say it doesn't matter what happens to me, my objective must be, to the best of my ability, to do whatever it takes.

There is no preparation for that. Nothing. So I sat down calmly and tried to analyse what most Australians needed to hear. I felt that they needed to hear a calming message, that everybody who is in a position to be making a difference is doing everything they could to secure the situation. I thought I was able to do that simply by being there and being as calm as I could. I remember being very conscious that I must've looked washed out because I'd been up the nights before dealing with the collapse of Ansett [a major airline group]. And I remember thinking I need to take a deep breath in order to send those calmer messages.

Leading people, teams and communities through periods of crisis is always a difficult aspect of leadership. Andrew Scipione talked about how he had to respond as the New South Wales police commissioner on 15 December 2014, when a lone gunman held 10 customers and eight employees hostage in the Sydney Lindt Café siege. During this time of crisis Andrew spoke of what guided his actions and communications, particularly with the public:

I had to make sure first and foremost that I always told the truth. If you try and lie to people – not only to the community, but to the media – they'll only fall for that once. Second, be very, very open. Within a crisis you cannot over communicate. Think about this. It's now six o'clock. Mary, who has gone to work and left mum and dad, isn't home yet. She should be home but she's not. And there's been a crisis in the city.

What would be enough communication, what would be enough information to them? If it doesn't compromise what we're doing, if it doesn't risk the event, then regular communication is important. If you want trust you've got to have relationship, and you cannot over communicate in a crisis. You then need to be very clear in what you're communicating. To call it as it is you need to be able to say: this is not going well or this will change, we will be coming back to you.

Three-quarters of what comes out in the first instance is blah, blah, blah, and people will grab hold of two or three things you say. You need to be telling people what it is they need to hear in very simple, straightforward messages.

All leaders are going to make mistakes, an organisation the size of ours with the complexity dealing with the issues that we do, from time to time we make mistakes. But when you've got that emotional bank account and you dig deep enough then the community can say you are doing your duty as best you could.

If you do that honestly and you do all those things you talked about, they'll give you credit if you fail. But if you have no account, they will write you off. They won't give you support. They won't listen to you.

These stories exemplify that when faced with difficult circumstances successful leaders step up and do what is needed for those they are leading. It might be uncomfortable and it might be difficult, but leaders who care for their teams and want to them thrive will step out of their comfort zone to help where help is needed.

'It is desirable that leaders bring intelligence, but it is essential that they exercise empathy. Leaders of head and heart are best placed to innovate amid disruption and engage across diversity.'

– McCRINDLE

THE CUSTOMER COMES SECOND

Many outstanding business leaders back the idea of the customer coming *second* and employees or workers coming *first*. One includes Simon Sinek, who said: 'Happy employees ensure happy customers. And happy customers ensure happy shareholders – in that order.' Sir Richard Branson said: 'I have always believed that the way you treat your employees is the way they will treat your customers, and that people flourish when they are praised.'

If leaders want to create thriving organisations and teams they will do well to look after their staff, prioritise their wellbeing and help them to thrive in their role. When employees are cared for there is a flow-on effect to both clients and the organisation.

EMPATHETIC LEADERS

Not only is *who* we are leading changing, but *when, where* and *how* we work is also undergoing massive transitions. An AlphaBeta report for Google Australia states it is our uniquely human skills that are needed to thrive as robotics and artificial intelligence change the nature of work. The report encourages workplace leaders and broader society to 'understand and embrace their roles in teaching skills that make us uniquely human: empathy, ingenuity, cooperation, resilience, ethics and integrity. Having these skills will allow future Australians to succeed in a world where human work will continue to be as indispensable as the machines that enable our society to function.'[5]

Our own report into the future of eduction[6] surveyed 1,002 parents of school-age children to find out their perceptions and expectations of schooling. Parents wanted schools as a priority to 'develop transferable skills' and also 'future proof students by equipping them with workforce skills' even above 'educating students to achieve high academic results'.

Preparing students for a global world and workforce is the key priority parents have. The anticipated rise of automation has led to a focus on developing 21st-century skills for lifelong learning in students. Within this context, parents believed students were most equipped with digital skills and creativity (60% and 57% respectively).

There is work to do, however, in the area of developing leadership qualities, with just 42% saying students are extremely/very equipped, followed by critical thinking with just 43% believing students are extremely or very equipped. As the world of work changes, it is the character qualities as well as competencies that will futureproof Generation Alpha.

A critical role of leadership is to motivate and inspire people towards a common goal or outcome, thus interpersonal and human skills are important when leading teams of people. The uniquely human skills of empathy, ingenuity, co-operation, resilience, ethics and integrity are all contained within emotional intelligence.

In our worker survey, more than seven in 10 workers (72%) stated that it is extremely or very important for a manager to possess emotional intelligence.

In his book *Emotional Intelligence*, thought leader Daniel Goleman describes how important emotional intelligence is in the workplace:

> The destructive effects of miserable morale, intimidated workers or arrogant bosses or any of the other deficiencies of emotional intelligences in the workplace can go largely unnoticed by those outside the immediate scene. But the cost can be read in signs such as decreased productivity, missed deadlines, mistakes and mishaps, and an exodus of employees to more congenial settings.

> There is, inevitably, a cost to the bottom line from low levels of emotional intelligence on the job. When it is rampant, companies can crash and burn. The cost effectiveness of emotional intelligence is a relatively new idea for business, one some managers may find hard to accept.

> In the corporate life of tomorrow, the basic skills of emotional intelligence will be ever more important in teamwork, in cooperation, in helping people learn together how to work

more effectively. As knowledge-based services and intellectual capital become more central to corporations, improving the way people work together will be a major way to leverage intellectual capital, making a critical competitive difference. To thrive, if not survive, corporations will do well to boost their collective emotional intelligence.[7]

It is desirable that leaders bring intelligence, but it is essential that they exercise empathy. Leaders of head and heart are best placed to innovate amid disruption and engage across diversity. Empathy is recognised as being a skill needed for the future. Much has been written about the increasing need for graduates in STEM – science, technology, engineering and mathematics – yet they will also require empathy skills. Hence the term 'STEMpathy', which combines the two needs.

Empathetic leadership is essential for helping people feel comfortable enough in an organisation to share new ideas and be creative and innovative. In our generational training we encourage the leaders of meetings to let the youngest person share first. Brené Brown says in her book on vulnerability, *Daring Greatly*: 'What's the most significant barrier to creativity and innovation? The fear of introducing an idea and being ridiculed, laughed at and belittled. If you are willing to subject yourself to that experience, and if you survive it, then it becomes the fear of failure and of being wrong. The problem is that often great ideas sound crazy and failure is needed. Learning and creating are inherently vulnerable.'[8]

Leaders who have empathy and emotional intelligence, who care about their teams and help them to thrive by creating safe spaces for them to share new ideas, step out of their comfort zone and fail, will help their organisations to thrive and succeed.

INSPIRING LEADERS

Five words that define this era's team members are: *digital*, in terms of the tools they use; *global*, in terms of the outlook or perspective they bring; *social*, in terms of who influences them and shapes their attitudes and decisions;

mobile, in terms of where they live, work and connect; and *visual*, in terms of how they process content.

Leaders need to motivate and lead in a world of message saturation and information overload, and in order to cut through they have to find engaging and innovative ways to connect and respond. An effective leader will take into account these four aspects of engagement:

❖ *Interest:* creating interest will gain the attention and focus of the team members. A popular saying in the education sphere states: 'When the student is ready the teacher will appear.' Learning can only occur when there is attention and the prerequisite of attention is interest. Leaders need to create interest in their teams before communicating tasks and objectives.

❖ *Instruction:* this is the stage where the leader delivers the content. A key focus of instruction is equipping the team to ensure the members are set up for success.

❖ *Involvement:* after the interest is gained and the instruction delivered, the team needs to be involved in applying the learning. The best leaders get their teams engaged in the work and collaborating towards an outcome.

❖ *Inspiration:* effective communication transitions the focus from what you want them to do to why it is important they do it. If the interest and instruction engage the head and involvement requires the hands, inspiration is of the heart. The communication of great leaders is both rational and emotional.

Another strategy leaders can use to inspire their teams is storytelling, as stories engage people. Author and business executive Seth Godin said: 'Marketing is no longer about the stuff you make but about the stories that you tell.' Using stories is an effective way for leaders to cut through message saturation to educate, engage, inspire and motivate their teams.

On the wall of our office is a simple, two-step description of what we are committed to as researchers, demographers and social analysts: 'Discovering the insights, telling the story'. Data can be influential and research transformative, but only if effectively communicated. This is best done by telling the data story through visual reports, infographics, powerful case studies, engaging presentations and interactive digital platforms. As civil rights activist Maya Angelou famously said: 'I've learned that people will forget what you said, people will forget what you did, but people will never forget how you made them feel.'

Thankyou co-founder Daniel Flynn once reiterated this in an interview when we asked him the question, '*How can a leader help people to be inspired, safe and fulfilled at work?*':

> Probably the simplest way to put it is stories, because in a story there is context and in context there is safety, even in the most uncertain times. In a story there is inspiration because it's a story that points back to vision, a story that points to where you're heading. I think it's an amazing thing when you tell stories as a leader and as you encourage people to tell stories: stories of the impact, stories of the work and stories of the win.
>
> Stories are powerful, and we can underestimate that as leaders because we don't have time for the story. It's my caution to myself and any other leader to never underestimate the value of a story in leading day to day.

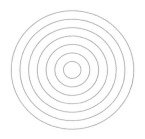

'Management is about persuading people to do things they do not want to do, while leadership is about inspiring people to do things they never thought they could.'

– STEVE JOBS

ENLARGING LEADERS

'A star wants to see himself rise to the top. A leader wants to see those around him rise to the top.' – Simon Sinek

Enlarging leaders know that workers, in their employment, are looking for opportunities to advance their careers, engage in professional development and work with purpose. Such leadership is more than being a great leader; it is about developing great leaders. Collaborative styles of leadership create a culture of leadership development by delegating both tasks and responsibility. These leaders see qualities in their staff they may not see in themselves; they back team members who don't even back themselves.

When a long-term leader departs and their organisation subsequently wanes, that is not a measure of their success but an indicator of their failure. Great leaders don't just have a succession plan, they have a succession queue – a depth of leaders they have trained. Leadership is defined by the culture created and the people developed.

From 2020 Generation Y and Generation Z, born since 1980, comprised the majority of the workforce, outnumbering Generation X and Baby Boomers for the first time. This demographic tipping point is transforming the world of work and leadership. Our research indicates that these generations respond most positively to a leadership style that creates a culture of enlarging the competence, character and people acuity of those being led.

Having wellbeing at work doesn't imply comfort, security, safety or ease, because if people are not being challenged or growing they will stagnate. While organisations should prioritise the health and safety of their workers in order to lead thriving teams, people also need to be challenged and given opportunities for growth. By our definition of growing, enlarging and stretching team members, wellbeing can't just be about protecting people from entering into stressful situations. We want people to experience testing in order for them to grow. People's natural sense is to avoid stress and hardships at all times but this creates dependency, which is the opposite from resilience. Enlarging leadership and prioritising the wellbeing of people is about growing them and their capacity.

In our worker survey we asked the question: *'When given a responsibility or a task outside of your comfort zone that stretches your capacity, which of the following best describes how you feel towards it?'* The majority of workers said that while they don't enjoy the process they know it grows them (53%), followed by 41% who said they enjoy the process and know it grows them and 6% who said they don't enjoy the process and don't find it helpful. The role of a leader is to ensure that people are being stretched in their capability even if they don't enjoy the process.

Ashley: Early in my career I was offered an opportunity to do a television interview for Sky News Business. I had only conducted one other TV interview before this, for 7 News Sydney. The 7 News interview was a pre-record in which they filmed some grabs of me talking about the topic. Even that interview was a big deal for me – I was so nervous about it – and this Sky News one was even more daunting. First because it was live and second because it was to be about 10 minutes in length, which is a long segment in the media world! Despite my nervousness I knew that if I didn't take the opportunity being presented to me I'd be missing an opportunity to grow. I also knew that if I didn't take it up I would regret it, and Mark and the rest of our team were encouraging me to just go for it.

So I did the interview. It involved a lot of preparation, but I felt it went well and afterwards I was so glad I did it. Now, having done a number of TV interviews since, both live and pre-recorded, I sit on the other side of the fence. I still participate in interviews, but I also encourage other team members to get involved when they pop up and often at the last minute. I encourage them and help them where I can with preparation. For me, the learning from this and many other similar experiences is to just do it, to have a go in spite of the fear. It reminds me of one of my favourite quotes from Sir Richard Branson: 'If someone offers you an amazing opportunity but you are not sure you can do it, say yes – then learn how to do it later!'

When leaders create environments for people to grow and contribute, not only do people flourish but the organisation benefits as well. As in a garden, healthy environments produce flourishing and thriving, and things grow. So how can leaders create such environments?

Encouraging

The first step to enlarge people within a team is to provide encouragement that builds people up and gives them the courage and support to try something new or step outside of their comfort zone. Traditional leadership styles where leaders barked orders to subordinates and commanded them are not cohesive to people's ability to flourish. Rather, when leaders take the time to encourage their teams and provide constructive feedback it creates an environment for people to grow both professionally and personally.

Here is some terrific advice about encouraging people:

I have always believed that the way you treat your employees is the way they will treat your customers, and that people flourish when they are praised.' – Sir Richard Branson, founder of Virgin Group

'When a manager recognizes an employee's behavior, personally and sincerely, both feel proud, gratified, and happy. There's a human connection that transcends the immediate culture to create a shared bond. The power of this bond is stronger than you might think; indeed, it's the power that holds together great organizational cultures.' – Erik Mosley and Derek Irvine, *The Power of Thanks: How Social Recognition Empowers Employees and Creates a Best Place to Work* (McGraw-Hill Education, 2015)

'Employees who report receiving recognition and praise within the last seven days show increased productivity, get higher scores from customers and have better safety records. They're just more engaged at work.' – Tom Rath, employee engagement consultant

'Nothing else can quite substitute for a few well-chosen, well-timed, sincere words of praise. They're absolutely free and worth a fortune.'
– Sam Walton, Walmart founder

Psychosomatic illness, in which our psychological state impacts upon our physical health, was recognised even in ancient times. Three thousand years ago King Solomon wrote: 'A cheerful heart is good medicine, but a broken spirit saps a person's strength' (Proverbs 17:22, New Living Translation).

Creating wellbeing at work requires more than just promoting physical health; mental health is pre-eminent. And something as simple as sincere, specific and consistent encouragement has a profound impact on emotional wellbeing.

When a leader takes the time to give encouragement and build up other team members those team members don't forget it. As Stephen Covey puts it, 'At some time in your life you probably had someone believe in you when you didn't believe in yourself', and this belief when expressed verbally is a powerful component of an enlarging leader.

Equipping

Some leaders are great at encouraging their teams, but it can't stop there. If people want to enlarge their teams they need to equip them with the necessary skills and training to make apt decisions. If leaders empower someone but don't train them they are exercising passive leadership, not enlarging leadership. A practical way leaders can better equip their team member is through helping them find and develop their strengths.

> **Ashley:** Over the last 12 months our team has invested in identifying and developing the unique strengths each member has. Every team member completed a survey that helped them to identify their unique strengths, and since then we have run other group and one-to-one sessions on how each of our

strengths are expressed in the workplace and beyond. The benefits of this have been twofold: individual team members are equipped with a better understanding of their unique strengths, and the rest of the team learns how to best work with that person in the work environment.

Entrusting

Entrusting team members can make a huge difference. A lot of leaders encourage and equip, but without delegating and entrusting the process, task or opportunity to the team people won't grow. Leaders often don't want to let go of things or delegate because they feel they can do the task better themselves, a barrier that prevents leaders from fully entrusting their teams with levels of responsibility.

In *Chapter One* Daniel Flynn says: 'You are someone's family, you are someone's friend and you are part of someone's team. In what ways do you show your family, friends or team members that you believe in them? Belief is a powerful thing. People achieve great things when they know that others believe they can.'[9]

Fear is a perennial enemy to individual and societal wellbeing and success. We witnessed with the coronavirus crisis of 2020 that fear of the unknown can lead to irrational responses such as panic buying and stockpiling. Our research showed that just 6% of shoppers engaged in deliberate stockpiling, which triggered another 30% to buy more than they ordinarily would. This led to the sustained supermarket shortages that impacted the majority of shoppers. In times such as these leaders of nations and organisations alike need to offer calm, confident, rational and practical messages.

Our research amid the COVID-19 situation asked Australians to rate the most important qualities of a leader in times of crisis. The most desired qualities were:

❖ Be completely open and honest in sharing information.

❖ Be prepared to make tough calls and make them early, and back yourself.

❖ Lead with strength and communicate confidence.

In his inauguration address in March 1933, during the ongoing Great Depression, Franklin D. Roosevelt offered such a message, relevant now as then:

> The only thing we have to fear is fear itself – nameless, unreasoning, unjustified terror which paralyses needed efforts to convert retreat into advance. In every dark hour of our national life a leadership of frankness and of vigour has met with that understanding and support of the people themselves, which is essential to victory. And I am convinced that you will again give that support to leadership in these critical days.

When leaders encourage, equip and then entrust people they empower them to overcome their fears, which creates the morale on which successful organisations are built.

In our national research into regrets, we found that when looking back over their lives almost two in three people (62%) said they wished they had taken more risks. When asked for the biggest regrets they have, among the most mentioned were 'not saying yes to more opportunities', 'always choosing the safe option' and 'not making the most of their life'.

When leaders enlarge the capacity of their teams, act as champions for them and encourage, equip and empower them to step outside their comfort zone and try new things, people will flourish.

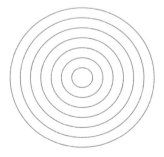

'Leadership is defined by the culture created and the people developed.'

– McCRINDLE

CREATING A CULTURE OF BELONGING

There is much talk in the current climate about diversity and embracing this aspect of our workplaces, communities and society at large. Diversity in the workplace is important for leaders because workplaces are at their best when they are representative of the broader communities in which they operate. If we aren't age diverse we're not connecting across the generations. If we aren't culturally diverse we don't represent the clients and customers we serve. If we don't have diversity of background, opinion and life stage then we can't best understand and serve our communities.

Our analysis is that people connect naturally with those within a seven-year older and younger age range. For example, if you are 40 years old, you will connect and relate best to those who are between the ages of 33 and 47. Interestingly, this 14-year age connectability lines up with the generational spans (15 years). In other words, we can relate most effortlessly to people within our generation or broad age group. Of course we can and should relate socially beyond this seven-year range, but it takes more effort to connect and engage.

Baby Boomers will require some intentionality to connect with their Millennial customers. Generation Z staff members have to make a deliberate effort to relate to their Generation X team members. It is self-evident therefore that Generation Z employees will better connect with Generation Z customers than Baby Boomers will, and vice versa. This is why it is ideal that workplaces have a range of different ages and people from different generations so they can better connect with a diverse range of customers and clients.

Here are two questions workplace leaders need to ask about the composition of their teams:

Do we represent our community/clients/customers?
and

Can we relate to our community/clients/customers?

Majority myopia is what we call malady of the majority group, which doesn't even recognise an under-representation of minority groups. For example, leaders in a company of mostly Anglo staff may not even realise there is an under-representation of culturally diverse staff members, but a would-be job applicant of Asian descent, for instance, will certainly notice it and may be less inclined to work there as a result, further entrenching the mono-culture.

When people feel as though they belong in a workplace and are valued, they have a greater chance of flourishing. When a workplace becomes a place of community, connection and belonging, people are attracted to the organisation, are more engaged at work and are retained for longer. Workplaces can be among the strongest of communities because members contribute to a common cause and are unified in the process. For communities, belonging is not dependant on contributing, but contributing enhances and fulfils people's belonging. When work is a place where we have a meaningful role, where we have authentic social connections, where we are aligned to the purpose and where we make a recognised contribution, we have a place of wellbeing for individuals and teams.

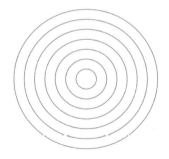

'Belonging is
not dependant
on contributing,
but contributing
enhances and
fulfils belonging.'

– McCRINDLE

LEADERS WHO EMBRACE VULNERABILITY

Over the last few years the idea of embracing imperfection and vulnerability in people's personal and professional lives has become mainstream, largely due to Brené Brown's extensive research on vulnerability and the power of it to make us more connected: 'Imperfections are not inadequacies; they are reminders that we're all in this together. Somehow we've come to equate success with not needing anyone. Many of us are willing to extend a helping hand, but we're very reluctant to reach out for help when we need it ourselves. It's as if we've divided the world into "those who offer help" and "those who need help." The truth is that we are both.'[10]

The co-founder of Pacific Equity Partners, Tim Sims, said that what makes a leader successful in an organisation is their ability to be transparent with their team about failings and shortcomings, to create an environment of transparency and trust:

> For 40 years I advised chief executives and large corporations on how to grow profits and share price. And we enjoyed great success in that business. For the last 20 years we've been buying businesses and appointing leaders to run them. On average those businesses have doubled their profits during the hold period.
>
> So, what attributes do those leaders who doubled the profits of companies have? If I had to extract a really interesting attribute of those leaders, those men and women are leaders with high energy who also have high emotional quotients and relate to people quite well. They have an ability to make rapid decisions after taking good counsel. They engage the people, explain the mission, make decisions. But the most important attribute they seem to have, the surprise, is that they are sufficiently secure enough that they are willing to reverse bad decisions – they are willing to admit when they make a wrong decision and fix it.
>
> What is remarkable about chief executives that make public errors and correct them is they make it acceptable, with humility,

for all people in the organisation to make an error and correct it. Two remarkable things happen if that is achieved. First, the organisational level of honesty and transparency is improved. You don't have to hide your errors anymore. And so if this executive is able to own up to making mistakes, it empowers others to own up to making mistakes.

It also unleashes a second powerful ingredient: it enables members of the organisation to try risky things, which enables people to contribute to the mission. They are willing to take some risk within reasonable control parameters and if they get it wrong they own up to it – this is the key thing that defines achieving organisations.

Leaders who are open and transparent with their staff and who are vulnerable and model this behaviour enable their teams to also be open and transparent. A lack of trust is a barrier to wellbeing, as trust enables people to connect and share successes and failures more openly. In our research that looked at the most desirable qualities of a leader, the top five qualities included not only 'making tough calls', 'leading with strength' and 'communicating confidence', but also 'showing compassion and empathy'.

It turns out that business is ultimately about people, and the people, if well led, deliver superior products, services and business outcomes. Enlarging leaders prioritise people. On the wall of our office in the midst of where our team members sit we have a statement that sums this up and keeps us focused on this value: 'People matter most. With our attitude, our words and our actions we value our team members, our clients and our community. We champion our team's ideas, insights and input and we celebrate each other's successes. In all we do we're committed to equipping, encouraging and enlarging people'.

'It turns out that business is ultimately about people, and the people, if well led, deliver superior products, services and business outcomes.'

– McCRINDLE

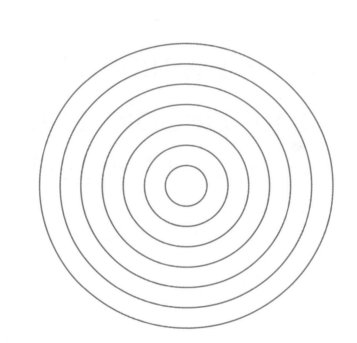

CHAPTER 8

WHY WORK
WELLBEING IS NON-
NEGOTIABLE

I n a world of screen saturation, 24/7 expectations and always-on technologies, people are seeking solace, ironically, through technology solutions, mindfulness apps and screen-time management to make their lives function more sustainably. The search for wellbeing, though, predates our era.

In January 1948 the Commonwealth Arbitration Court in Australia gave official assent to the 40-hour, five-day working week. The public push for this work/life balance was synonymous with the symbol '888': eight hours' work, eight hours' recreation and eight hours' sleep. However, more than seven decades on, it seems that this balance has eluded most Australians. The latest census[1] results shows we are still working long hours in paid employment, with two in five employed Australians working beyond the eight-hour day and way beyond it when commute time is included. Sleep studies continue to show that most Australians average an hour less than the ideal eight-hour goal, and the average discretionary time enjoyed by working Australians is 3.5 hours per day – well below the goal of eight.[2] Even the structure of a working week has faded in an era with gig economy jobs, shiftwork and flexible hours and days.

Instructions for wellbeing go back to the most ancient writings. The creation narrative records the six days of creation, and on the seventh day God rested. The Jewish Torah and the Old Testament scriptures record the Ten Commandments, of which the fourth is to keep a day of rest: 'Six days you shall labor and do all your work, but the seventh day is a sabbath … On it you shall not do any work' (Deuteronomy 5:12-13).

> **Mark:** As a young child I would enjoy getting out of church after the service to play cricket in the car park with my friends, only to be roused on each Sunday by dear Mr Murray, who would walk past grimly, shaking his head and saying: 'Playing sport on the sabbath – you boys should be ashamed of yourselves.' Needless to say it was a pretty conservative church. But I was pleased to read a few years later that to those who burdened the day of rest with pious restrictions, Jesus gave this corrective: 'The Sabbath was made to meet the needs of people, and not people to meet the requirements of the Sabbath.' (Mark 2:27 NLT).

Amid our culture of burnout, workplace stress, the office in our pocket and always-on technology, reinstituting work and rest rhythms are imperative. Note that the 6 + 1 formula of work and rest is not designed as a strategy by which to achieve more productive work. Wellbeing requires times to engage actively in the world of work and time to enjoy, in gratitude, the world of rest and play.

This is very relevant in our work context where, as reported by the ABS, 36% of Australian men and 45% of Australian women say they are always or often rushed or pressed for time.[3] It seems the human need to have weekly seasons of work and rest is hardwired into us, and when we push against it wellbeing is diminished.

Work wellbeing is also constrained if our employment is viewed simply as a means of earnings. The 40 hours of work per week that are standard for many comprise more than one third (36%) of the 112 waking hours each week brings. Indeed, 40 hours per week over 48 working weeks annually across a working life that extends from the early 20s to the late 60s equates to more than 90,000 hours.

Such a significant investment of our lives must then be a means of finding purpose, meeting social needs and having a societal impact. Our research shows that the size of the employer, the employer brand or the remuneration alone are not the key attraction factors for young workers today. Rather, the fulfilling job role, career pathway, workplace culture, organisational values and an engaging management style are key to attracting and retaining the new generations of staff. These are all factors of wellbeing.

Wellbeing must be a key issue in Australian workplaces as workers are expecting it to be a priority and are even willing to forgo other perks in order to achieve greater wellbeing. According to a McCrindle/Reventure survey of workers, one in four Australian workers (25%) would sacrifice company perks for better wellbeing in their workplace, and one in five would sacrifice a promotion (21%) or a pay rise (19%). Stressed workers would more readily sacrifice company perks (28%) and a pay rise (27%) for better wellbeing in their workplace.[4] Prioritising the wellbeing of employees will help both individuals and organisations to thrive and flourish.

The reality is that the world of work has changed. We have moved to a predominantly knowledge-based economy where an employee's value comes from their ability to think and manipulate information as opposed to moving or creating physical objects. The composition of the workforce has changed, with Generations Y and Z now comprising more than half the global workforce. Leadership styles have changed, with command and control leaders being replaced by leaders who collaborate and contribute. Workplaces need to adapt and respond, so that workers are looked after while also being mentally stretched and grown in capacity in an environment in which they can flourish and thrive.

ATTRACTION AND RETENTION

It has never been harder to attract, recruit and retain staff. The workforce, along with the population, is ageing, and young people are staying in education longer. Even in these economically subdued times the unemployment rate remains relatively low, and below what it was in the early 1990s.[5]

Further contributing to an employees' market is the increased number of options available when it comes to vocation. There are more post-education options than ever before for young people: opportunities to travel, work overseas or retrain for another career. The emerging generation of employees isn't just thinking about their local area, state or nation, but have a global perspective in terms of where they can work, study and travel.

Also, it is the era of the gig economy, contingent work, freelancing and entrepreneurism. A national Triple J study[6] found that one in three 18 to 29 year olds had a 'side hustle', so while we may think about the emerging generation as employees they may well be employers at the same time.

Twenty-first-century life is rarely linear and sequential. Traditionally, a person completes the education stage, moves into the working years and then perhaps after a career change or two heads into retirement. Now it is more a mosaic of different roles, phases and careers, with the education phase extending well into adulthood and throughout the work life. This multi-career generation may retrain several times and find their careers taking them to other states and countries.

Based on the average tenure of staying with an employer for two years and nine months,[7] if we project this out over the lifetime of today's school leaver they will have at least 18 jobs across six careers! In a big shift from a career for life, it is not unusual for multiple job holders to have several careers in a day! This new reality of portfolio careers and shorter tenure means employers will need to be more efficient at recruiting and training staff. Based on this average tenure, employers who are still conducting three-year graduate programs will find that more than half of their employees will not stay long enough to complete the program. Even two-week induction courses are being reduced to two days. The one-day training session may now be run over a couple of hours, online or on the job.

The huge decline in tenure is often attributed to a character flaw in the emerging generations. However, the cause is not a lack of loyalty or a poor work ethic; it is simply a response to changed times. The new recruits have come of age in an era of disappearing industries, outsourcing, offshoring, downsizing and contracting. Traditional industries are disappearing, many roles are being replaced by technology and job security has diminished. Generation Z are playing to the new rules of the employment world.

As we have explored, if workers' wellbeing isn't prioritised the next generation will move on. In an era where there are more vacant jobs than viable candidates, the interviewees are assessing the employers, not the other way around. When we hear reports from organisations that have young graduates burning out before they are fully inducted in, that is an indicator of a poor work environment. A focus on work wellbeing will not only improve the culture, it will reduce the turnover: which is one of the biggest business costs.

FUTURE PROOFING YOUR CAREER

With the realities of massive change facing individuals, organisations and sectors, many are thinking about how they can future proof their career. Often the conversation becomes very technical in terms of the jobs that will exist and the skills people will need to thrive in times of change. While it is an important topic, the bigger issue around future proofing careers is *wellbeing*. What matters when talking about the future of your career is that there is wellbeing in your life, that you are in it for the long haul.

The fact that people hold multiple jobs across different careers will only be accelerated for emerging generations. Additionally, the retirement age in Australia is pushing into the 70s. This is a long way from what it used to be, when many people had retired by age 60. To run such a work marathon and run it well means people have to be both physically well and holistically well – which embraces social, relational, mental, financial, vocational and spiritual aspects.

Workplace health and safety initiatives such as zero-harm policies, safety lighting, anti-slip surfaces and no-trip hazards are standard in a workplace. Workplaces routinely implement ergonomic features such as supportive chairs, monitor positioning and standing desks. Our research on remote working found that for those with flexible arrangements, their most dangerous workday was when they worked from home due to the non-ergonomic home office and slip and trip hazards!

For many workers today the biggest wellbeing impediments are mental, not physical. These include: toxic feedback from clients or customers or within the team; stress; unreasonable deadlines; multiple priorities being juggled; general pressure; the increasing expectations of customers; shorter timeframes in which people want a response or a service to be delivered; and people needing to deliver more with less. All of these have the potential to create hazards mentally and, as we have seen, impact physically.

In the knowledge economy people may still be able to work if they have physical ailments because they are not swinging shovels or working on the factory floor, but people are impaired in their work if they are not fit mentally. When we think about our long-term physical health we no doubt have a goal of not only avoiding illness but also living with wellness, and what best supports this is fitness. So it is with us mentally. As a basic we want to have a lifestyle that will prevent mental illness and we want to manage stress to support mental wellness, but to give improved protection and resilience we need to develop mental fitness. Just as regular exercise improves physical fitness, so will proactive wellbeing practices build mental fitness. As a wise leader said to us recently, 'Find out what refreshes and nurtures your soul and do lots of it.'

In our worker survey we asked the question: *How big an impact do you think the following will have on the future of work?* Of the seven factors we tested, 'mental health and stress of workers' was the factor that workers believed would have the biggest impact, with more than three in five workers (62%) saying it would have a significant or large impact. This was followed by demographic trends (such as the ageing population, which 55% of workers said would have a significant or large impact), the physical workspace and where work will be done (55%), sectors disappearing (52%), computerisation of robotics (52%), global workforce trends (46%) and the gig economy (41%).

From demographic shifts to technological advancements the future of work is changing, yet it is already being recognised that the health and stress of workers – wellbeing – is an essential factor that will impact and define the future of work.

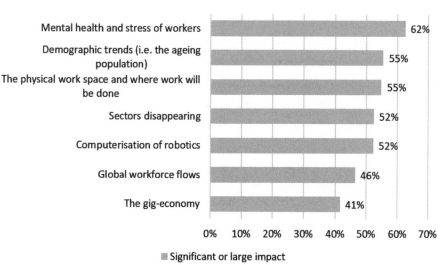

How big of an impact do you think the following will have on the future of work?

Mental health and wellbeing are more important than physical wellbeing when it comes to thriving in the current world of work. For physical health reasons COVID-19 ushered in social isolation, yet there have been flow-on mental health implications from this. In this new world of increased remote working it is essential that leaders connect with their teams and facilitate social interaction even when there's not the connection point of the workplace. The phrase of this era, 'social distancing', requires in response a focus on team connecting. If people don't future proof their working life through mental wellbeing it will have significant financial implications for themselves and for the economy at a macro level.

RETURN ON INVESTMENT

'The servant-leader is a servant first. It begins with the natural feeling that one wants to serve. Then conscious choice brings one to aspire to lead. The best test is: do those served grow as persons?' – Robert K. Greenleaf

If organisations and leaders invest time in ensuring their workers are engaged, energised and enthusiastic, that investment will come back to them. If people enjoy what they do they will experience less stress and will give their best selves. In *Thrive*, Arianna Huffington said: 'Increasingly, companies are realising that their employees' health is one of the most important predictors of the company's health.' She delves into the idea that 'a healthy workforce is a productive workforce', and that companies that invest in the health and wellbeing of their staff experience 'higher worker engagement, lower healthcare costs, higher productivity and lower absenteeism'.[8]

The correlation between a focus on employee wellbeing and engagement, retention and advocacy also proved true in our research when we asked the question in our worker survey: *'Does your workplace have a commitment to the wellbeing of its employees?'* Sadly, three in 10 (30%) concluded no, with 'yes definitely' (24%) and 'yes, to some extent' (46%) comprising the rest.

When we analysed the respondents in the yes and no category across the other questions in the survey, the correlations were fascinating and consistent. Commitment to the wellbeing of employees had a direct impact on their likelihood of making the same choice about their current workplace, their engagement in their workplace, how likely they would be to recommend their workplace to others and – if it were up to them – how likely they would be to still be working in their current place of employment in two years' time.

We asked a number of pertinent questions, as follows.

*'On a scale of 0 to 10, if you had **the chance to re-make your choice to work in your current workplace**, how likely is it that you would make the same choice?'*

	LOW COMMITMENT TO WELLBEING OF EMPLOYEES	A COMMITMENT TO WELLBEING OF EMPLOYEES	REPEATER SCORE INCREASE
Promoter (score of 9 or 10)	12%	34%	2.8 x

*'Thinking about **how engaged you are in your current workplace and role**, on a scale of 0 to 10 please rate your current engagement with your job.'*

	LOW COMMITMENT TO WELLBEING OF EMPLOYEES	A COMMITMENT TO WELLBEING OF EMPLOYEES	ENGAGEMENT SCORE INCREASE
Promoter (score of 9 or 10)	11%	34%	3.1 x

*'On a scale from 0 to 10, **how likely is it that you would recommend your organisation as a place to work**, where relevant, to a friend or contact?'*

	LOW COMMITMENT TO WELLBEING OF EMPLOYEES	A COMMITMENT TO WELLBEING OF EMPLOYEES	CULTURE SCORE INCREASE
Promoter (score of 9 or 10)	8%	34%	4.3 x

*'If it were up to you, on a scale of 0 to 10, **how likely is it that you would still be working in your current place of employment in two years' time?'***

	LOW COMMITMENT TO WELLBEING OF EMPLOYEES	A COMMITMENT TO WELLBEING OF EMPLOYEES	TENURE SCORE INCREASE
Promoter (score of 9 or 10)	15%	39%	2.6 x

A commitment to worker wellbeing leads to greater satisfaction across a number of personal areas, including:

	LOW COMMITMENT TO WELLBEING OF EMPLOYEES*	A COMMITMENT TO WELLBEING OF EMPLOYEES*	LIFE SATISFACTION INCREASE
Relationships	41%	60%	1.5 x
My life overall	29%	55%	1.9 x
Your work life	21%	51%	2.4 x
Personal fulfilment	28%	48%	1.7 x
Work/life balance	22%	48%	2.2 x
Physical wellbeing/ health	24%	42%	1.8 x
Sleep patterns	22%	39%	1.8 x
Connected in the community	20%	36%	1.8 x
Financial situation	19%	36%	1.9 x
Making a difference in the world around me	18%	36%	2.0 x
*% extremely or very satisfied			

A workplace's commitment to wellbeing can also have an impact on their workers' sense of meaning in life, with 84% of workers whose workplaces have a commitment to the wellbeing of their employees saying they definitely or somewhat had a sense of meaning in life, compared with 60% of workers whose workplaces did not have a commitment to worker wellbeing.

Workers in workplaces that *do* have a commitment to the wellbeing of their employees are more likely to agree with a range of statements about positive workplace community than those whose workplaces *do not* have a commitment to the wellbeing of employees.

'To what extent do you agree with the following statements about your workplace community?'

	LOW COMMITMENT TO THE WELLBEING OF EMPLOYEES*	A COMMITMENT TO THE WELLBEING OF EMPLOYEES*	WORK SATISFACTION INCREASE
I have a high level of trust in the people I work with	30%	66%	2.2 x
Everyone works together effectively, particularly when trying to accomplish difficult goals	28%	66%	2.4 x
I feel good about working in my current workplace	20%	66%	3.3 x
People care about each other and treat each other with respect	24%	65%	2.7 x
There are systems to ensure employee wellbeing	9%	65%	7.2 x
People are generally interested in their work	30%	64%	2.1 x
The workplace is diverse and representative of the broader community	28%	63%	2.3 x
I feel invested in as a worker	18%	62%	3.4 x
It feels like a community where people support each other beyond just getting the work done	17%	60%	3.5 x
*% extremely or very satisfied			

Workplaces that have a commitment to employee wellbeing are also having impacts on other aspects of workers' lives outside the workplace, such as a sense of purpose and their ability to make a difference in the lives of others.

'Other than to get paid, how important is your work in contributing to the following areas?'

	LOW COMMITMENT TO THE WELLBEING OF EMPLOYEES*	A COMMITMENT TO THE WELLBEING OF EMPLOYEES*	SELF-ACTUALISATION INCREASE
A sense of purpose	47%	70%	1.5 x
To develop me as a person	44%	66%	1.5 x
To make a difference in the lives of others	38%	66%	1.7 x
To better society and the world	37%	63%	1.7 x
A sense of community and belonging	35%	62%	1.8 x
*% extremely or very satisfied			

Those in a workplace that *did not* have a commitment to the wellbeing of its employees were also more likely to say that leadership was a blocker to them thriving at work (41%), compared with 20% of those in a workplace with a commitment to employee wellbeing. Similarly, those in a workplace with a commitment to employee wellbeing were more likely to say the leader of the team had a significant or large impact than those whose workplaces did not have this same commitment to wellbeing (70% compared with 58%). Former police commissioner Andrew Scipione spoke about how crucial the focus on wellbeing for workers is, particularly in a vocation such as policing:

If we're serious about the wellbeing of our teams then they need to see the commitment of your lips is matched by the commitment of your deeds. The organisation that I was a part of by its very nature breaks people. You're expecting people to do things that really humans shouldn't have to do. You see the very worst of people that will shock you at first and then numb you later.

We need to overly protect our people because they are our greatest asset. Without them we have nothing. So we put together a safety command that not only did its best to try and put people back together, but even more so to try and prevent what was happening in the first place.

We recruited a lot of psychologists, physios and medical staff. We set up gymnasiums, counselling areas and areas where people could seek support once a day or three times a week to get a plan and a program with experts working with them. These are the sort of things that, once you do them, people start to see that you really do care, you are genuine.

And then we said, hang on a minute, this responsibility doesn't just stop once these people leave the force. Because, you know, we might have got 10 or 15 years' service, but they're broken for life. So we actually then put together a group working with the police legacy to continue to do the same after they finish with us. It's like with family: even though your family members don't live in your house any more, they are still family.

Part of our cultural change was getting them to understand that our responsibility doesn't finish just because you're no longer part of the organisation. So we would set up days where retired officers would come into the station to be part of what was their life for 20, 30 or 40 years.

It is well known by military, police, paramedic and other first responder organisations that the work their team members on the front lines do often leads to emotional numbness, detachment and avoidance behaviours. This is also true of nurses, doctors, aged care workers, those in social support services and child protection who deal with poverty, abuse, trauma and the vulnerable. Yet from teachers to charity workers, from lawyers to case managers, from carers to those in the health-care sector, there can be mental health impacts from the work role that employers need to be aware of.

The leading cause of death in Australia and many developed nations is ischaemic heart disease, which results from a reduced blood supply to the heart muscle. However, even more prevalent than the disease of the physical heart is damage to the emotional, spiritual one. Physical heart disease is also mental and emotional, and is harder to diagnose and detect as the symptoms are more subtle. Emotional heart disease is not a sclerosis or hardening of coronary arteries, but a hardening of the heart towards family, friends, colleagues and ultimately oneself.

This hardening can happen to people who are committed to their job, who function well in their life and are seemingly happy. It happens slowly, subtly, in response to pain, hard times, unresolved conflict and relational disconnection and workplace stress. Good leaders observe the signs in their teams and look out for the symptoms in their own lives as well. When organisations demonstrate they care about people outside of work, just as they do when they're on the job, work wellbeing will ensue. 'Above all else, guard your heart, for everything you do flows from it.' (Proverbs 4:23, NLT).

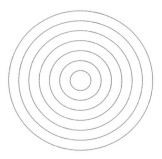

'Not finance. Not strategy. Not technology. It is teamwork that remains the ultimate competitive advantage, both because it is so powerful and so rare.'

– PATRICK LENCIONI

THE POWER OF THE TEAM

Wellbeing at work is enhanced by teamwork, which results in greater productivity and performance and provides opportunities for social connection and shared celebrations. The ability to work together and draw upon each other's strengths is one significant aspect missing from the lives of those who work remotely or are not part of a consistent team.

In *Chapter One* Daniel Flynn talks about the importance of the team, stating that people who come to Thankyou always commented on the culture, which had been established by 'ensuring they get the right people on the bus':

> Pulling a team together is one thing but working as a team is the next challenge. Modern society is pretty good at setting the agenda for workplace hierarchies. We naturally position a CEO or MD right up at the top of the chain and then proceed to rank all other roles according to importance in a neat reporting line below that. When you truly honour the gifts and talents that each team member has – instead of their organisational rank – then you develop unity in your own team that will position you to achieve incredible things.[9]

Mark: In my psychology training, I remember one lab experiment where three students were individually asked to pull on a rope attached to a scale that measured force. The competitive nature of these students meant they each tried their hardest to get the best score. After each of the individual scores was recorded, the three students were then asked to grab hold of the rope and together pull as hard as they could. Each time this experiment was performed, when the three pulled on the rope together the score was greater than when the three scores of the same individuals were totalled. This outcome illustrated to me the power of synergy: that 1 + 1 + 1 can equal four, five or even more!

When a team works together there is an additional factor in the result: the esprit de corps, or the dynamic of the team spirit, motivating each other, working so as to not let the others down, learning from the technique of the other and taking inspiration from each other. The best leaders understand the psychology of teams, the dynamic of social connection and the power of serving. They know that more important than a vision for the organisation is a vision for the team. Their teams are relationally functioning and high performing because they have a team-centric rather than a numbers-centric perspective.

'More important
than a vision for
the organisation
is a vision for
the team.'

– McCRINDLE

CHAPTER 9

HOW TO BE A WORK WELLBEING CHAMPION

When it comes to prioritising work wellbeing, all employees (including leaders) can play a part in implementing aspects of increasing workers' ability to flourish and thrive. As Simon Sinek reminds us: 'Leading is not the same as being the leader. Being the leader means you hold the highest rank, either by earning it, good fortune or navigating internal politics. Leading, however, means that others willingly follow you – not because they have to, not because they are paid to, but because they want to.'

In his book *Emotional Intelligence* Daniel Goleman said:

> The stars of an organisation are often those who have thick connections on all networks. Whether communications, expertise or trust. Beyond the master of these informal networks, other mastery of these included effectively coordinating their efforts in teamwork, being leaders in building consensus,

being able to see things from the perspective of others, such as customers or others on a work team, persuasiveness, and promoting cooperation while avoiding conflicts. While all of these rely on social skills, the stars also displayed another kind of knack. Taking initiative, being self-motivated enough to take on responsibilities above and beyond their stated job and self-management in the sense of regulating their time and work commitments well. All such skills of course are aspects of emotional intelligence. To thrive, if not survive, corporations will do well to boost their collective emotional intelligence.[1]

What this tells us is that those who know how to work with people, how to help their teams thrive and flourish and how to lead their organisations through times of rapid change are well positioned for the future. According to Dr Lindsay McMillan this has to begin with leadership, but every organisation needs people beyond the leaders who will champion it:

> Leadership has to be genuine, authentic, and communicate that we do care sincerely for our people. We must recognise that they are more than just a person that comes to work, because there's no beginning or end of work these days. Elements like giving parents' time to go to pick up their kids is huge. It needs to come through by changing the language and talking about some of the things that are more important to people than just completing the task.

> You've also got to find a champion within the organisation beyond the leader, who really champions the notion and champions the idea. When you have champions, you can actually see people getting good by just being around them, their enthusiasm is compelling.

ENGAGEMENT STRATEGY

How can people be a work wellbeing champion? What are some of the ways we can increase engagement in our workplaces and help each other to thrive?

After conducting many research projects across the different generations we developed an engagement strategy to help organisations prioritise the wellbeing and engagement of their teams. Organisations and people within them who implement the engagement strategy can help themselves and their colleagues and co-workers to thrive at work.

In our research of workers we discovered many factors that led to attracting and retaining workers and creating a culture of wellbeing, but here are the top five:

1. Workplace culture

2. Work/life integration

3. Varied job roles

4. Leadership style

5. Training

1. Workplace culture

Workplace culture, being multifactorial, is complex to define and measure. The origins of the word 'culture' come from the Latin *cultus*, which means 'care', and from the French *colere*, which means 'to till' (as in till the ground). There are many terms that stem from the word culture.[2] Anthropologists use the term to describe how people live. Our sociological definition is this: workplace culture is the set of answers to the reason for existence of our industry, organisation, team and role. At its simplest, culture is often described by the phrase 'It's how we do things around here.' It's the character and personality, the procedures and values, the purpose and ambition, the structures and traditions and the pattern of behaviour of the people and the organisation. It is the *who* of the organisation, the *how* they do it and importantly the *why*.

The biggest part of a workplace culture is the community of people who comprise the organisation. In her book *Daring Greatly*, Brené Brown said she believes 'We have to completely re-examine the idea of engagement. To reignite creativity, innovation and learning, leaders must re-humanise education and work. Learning how to engage with vulnerability and recognising and combatting shame.'[3]

Sir Ken Robinson, whose TED talk 'Do schools kill creativity?' is one of the most watched of all time, addresses the power of making this shift to replace the outdated idea that human organisations should work like machines with a metaphor that captures the realities of humanity. In his book *Out of Our Minds* he elaborates: 'However seductive the machine metaphor may be for industrial production, human organisations are not mechanisms and people are not components in them. People have values and feelings, perceptions and opinions, motivations and biographies. Whereas cogs and sprockets do not. An organisation is not the physical facilities within which it operates. It is the networks of people in it.'[4]

A key aspect of people achieving work wellbeing is their ability to feel connected to the people with whom they work, to feel they belong to the community the workplace creates. We posed a series of statements to Australian workers to gauge the general sentiment workers have towards their workplace community. Positively, more than half of workers (55%) agreed they have a high level of trust with the people they work with. Similarly, 53% agreed that people in their workplace cared about each other and treated each other with respect. While 55% agreed that everyone works together effectively, particularly when trying to accomplish difficult goals, 47% agreed that their workplace felt like a community where people supported each other beyond just getting the work done.

Although it is positive that almost half of workers (47%) agreed their workplace felt like a community, out of the 19 statements about the workplace we tested this one had the lowest percentage of respondents who strongly or somewhat agreed with it. This shows us that workplaces, organisations and leaders have an opportunity to help their teams connect with those they work with on a deeper level, rather than just collaborating around projects to get the work done.

In our years of social research and generational analysis one of our most requested presentation topics has been 'Understanding and Engaging Generation Z' (those born between 1995 and 2009). The oldest Generation Zs are now entering our workplaces, and within the next decade they will comprise a third of our global workforce. Generation Z is a very different generation when compared with generations past: they are the most formally educated, the most technologically savvy, the most materially endowed and the most globally connected generation ever.

While there are notable differences that leaders would do well to understand, anyone from any generation is a human first. As Dr Seuss put it: 'A person's a person, no matter how small.' Generation Z have the same intrinsic human needs we all have: to be accepted, to belong and to be part of a community. These are timeless yearnings, true of people in any place across any era. As psychologist Carl Rogers wrote: 'What is most personal is most universal.'

Workplaces are not just the places we come to do our work and then go home; they provide a unique opportunity for us to connect with others with whom we have commonality and spend the largest part of our day. At a time when face-to-face interaction is down, when screen-based communities are on the rise and when mental health has never been more talked about or more prevalent, workplaces can fulfil an intrinsic human need that can help individuals, teams and societies to thrive and flourish.

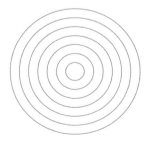

To what extent do you agree with the following statements about your workplace community?

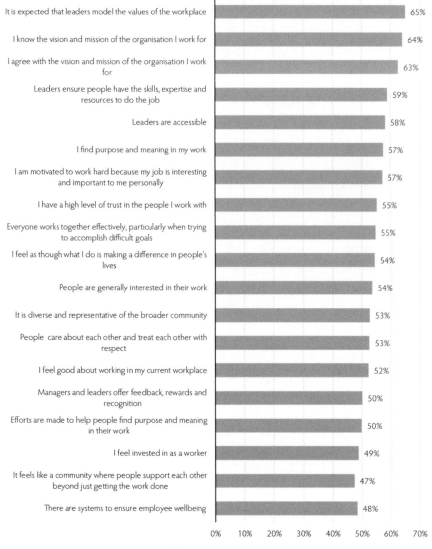

Strongly or somewhat agree

Statement	%
It is expected that leaders model the values of the workplace	65%
I know the vision and mission of the organisation I work for	64%
I agree with the vision and mission of the organisation I work for	63%
Leaders ensure people have the skills, expertise and resources to do the job	59%
Leaders are accessible	58%
I find purpose and meaning in my work	57%
I am motivated to work hard because my job is interesting and important to me personally	57%
I have a high level of trust in the people I work with	55%
Everyone works together effectively, particularly when trying to accomplish difficult goals	55%
I feel as though what I do is making a difference in people's lives	54%
People are generally interested in their work	54%
It is diverse and representative of the broader community	53%
People care about each other and treat each other with respect	53%
I feel good about working in my current workplace	52%
Managers and leaders offer feedback, rewards and recognition	50%
Efforts are made to help people find purpose and meaning in their work	50%
I feel invested in as a worker	49%
It feels like a community where people support each other beyond just getting the work done	47%
There are systems to ensure employee wellbeing	48%

Ashley: A couple of years ago we had a Generation Z member in our team who brought such a fun energy to the workplace. He introduced us to bitmojis, various slang terms and other Generation Z trends. As social researchers we have a particular interest in studying the generations, and it is always refreshing to have people of different generations in our team. Although I am of the generation just before Generation Z there is still such a big generation gap when it comes to the trends that shaped this generation, and how quickly these trends change!

One of the things I most enjoyed about having this particular Generation Z in our team was the fact that when he left the office at the end of the day he would often say: 'See-you later, fam.' 'Fam' (derived from family) is a slang term that refers to the people in your life with whom you're particularly close: your friends or those you can trust dearly. So the fact that he used the word to speak about his work colleagues was very special and showed that he not only enjoyed working with us as his colleagues, but that he viewed us as his friends and people he could trust.

As discussed in Chapter 2, our workplaces are reflective of a changing world. People are less likely to know their neighbours or be involved with community groups such as places of worship or their local clubs. This is even truer for the younger generations, who are delaying traditional life markers such as moving out of home, getting married or having children. Consequently, people look for multiple needs such as social connection and belonging to be met through their workplace. While workplaces can't fulfil every need, when people feel that work is a place where they belong it can help them to thrive.

In her extensive work on shame and vulnerability Brené Brown said: 'We are biologically, cognitively, physically, and spiritually wired to love, be loved, and to belong. When those needs are not met, we don't function as we were meant to be. We break. We fall apart. We numb. We ache … The absence of love and belonging will always lead to suffering.'

The relationships we have with others at work are a contributing factor to employee engagement. In our worker survey, more than three in five workers (65%) considered 'relationship with peers/colleagues' as extremely or very important in their place of employment. This was only second to workplace wellbeing, which 72% of workers said was extremely or very important in their place of employment. The ability to interact socially and work collaboratively was also considered important, with three in five (60%) citing a collaborative work environment as an extremely or very important part of their current or potential workplace.

A few years ago we conducted research into the concept of teleworking, which together with telecommuting are concepts that have been around since the early 1970s. At a time when flexible working conditions were beginning to emerge as an important must-have offer for organisations, we decided to investigate how workers felt about the concept of working remotely rather than commuting to a central place of work such as an office building, site, warehouse or store. This research is all the more relevant in the post-COVID-19 environment, where remote working has become a daily reality for more workers than ever before.

Our research found that Australians are eager to make significant changes to their working styles, embracing the freedom to work from home or remotely to their primary location of work. Four in five workers (80%) stated they would be more likely to stay longer with an existing employer should that employer provide them with the flexibility of working remotely or from home. More than half (52% of men and 51% of women) said they would be prepared to forgo a percentage of their pay in exchange for greater flexibility in their working arrangements.

Flexibility is important, yet in terms of culture and output our survey revealed that people do want and need the connection, collaboration and community that come from working with other people. The majority of Australians value the group collective, stating the importance of promoting the best team outcomes and setting aside times for gathering and brainstorming. Over two-thirds (68%) stated that the culture and output of a workplace is best when everyone is working in one place with a degree of flexibility for teleworking, or when there is a time for gathering and working together but also a significant time for working remotely. Only one in 10 (10%) said that productivity is best when workers work independently with occasional gathering, and very few (4%) reported seeing no need for workers to gather in order to achieve maximum output or develop cultural cohesion.

Another part of workplace community that is important to belonging is for workplaces to be reflective of the broader society in which they operate. As explored in Chapter 2, our society is culturally and generationally diverse and our workplaces should be reflective of this. Additionally, individuals and teams will be better placed to thrive when they feel their organisation embraces diversity. Just over half of workers (53%) strongly or somewhat agreed that their workplace was diverse and representative of the broader community. While this is positive, we have some way to go until the vast majority are able to say their workplace is representative of the broader community.

One aspect of diverse workplaces that most leaders are attuned to is gender representation in organisations, and particularly on boards and in positions of leadership. Women comprise almost half (47%) of Australia's workforce. More than two in five employed Australians (44%) strongly or somewhat agreed that not having enough flexible working options holds back Australian workplaces from achieving 50% women in senior leadership roles, followed by a lack of support for women exiting the workplace for family reasons (41% strongly or somewhat agreed). Work wellbeing will be enhanced in our workplaces when organisations, boards and governance are reflective of the society in which they operate.

Diversity is important for wellbeing and should be encouraged and given consideration in the workplace. Workplace teams and communities need to be united for a common goal, being the objectives of the organisation. Focusing on diversity is the first step in a multi-step approach. How can we align towards the goals and outcomes and find unity in diversity? It goes back to the idea that community is defined by its centre, by its focal point, not its circumference or boundaries that define who is in and who is out. Clarity is needed at the core of workplace communities: it should be clear what we are being aligned towards, the values and vision that unite and the purpose and mission that motivate.

When a workplace becomes a place of community, connection and belonging, not only are people attracted to the organisation, they are more engaged at work and are retained for longer. When we feel that work is a place that we belong and in which we have deep social connections, and where there is an authentic sense of community, we have a greater ability to thrive as individuals and to thrive as teams.

2. Work/life integration

> 'For a long time it had seemed to me that life was about to begin – real life. But there was always some obstacle in the way. Something to be got through first, some unfinished business, time still to be served, a debt to be paid. Then life would begin. At last it dawned on me that these obstacles were my life.'
> – Alfred D'Souza

For most of us, our employment matters and it is a major part of our lives. However, it is not our whole life. A career that allows workers the opportunity to continue other aspects of their life stage, whether they be educational, social, spiritual or entrepreneurial, will be highly attractive. In our worker survey, more than one in five (22%) said the main reason they left their previous employment situation was because of the lack of a work/life balance.

The term 'work/life balance' is a concept often used in 21st-century workplaces and particularly for Generation Ys, those born between 1980 and 1995. This generation grew up in a time shaped by the emergence of digital technology, laptop computers, the internet and the sharing economy, which had significant impacts on the workforce by enabling work to be done anywhere, any time, further blurring the lines of work and rest. Generation Y is the generation of Mark Zuckerberg (Facebook founder), Evan Spiegel (Snapchat founder), Daniel Ek (Spotify founder) and Drew Houston (Dropbox founder), all of whom exemplify work flexibility, entrepreneurism and a belief that anything is possible.

> **Ashley:** I recently heard a conference speaker talking about the Millennial generation and their expectations of the workforce. The speaker mentioned his 23-year-old son, who had just finished his studies and was about to enter the workforce. He was excited to begin interviewing, and when asked about job prospects the son told his father that he was looking forward to finding a job where he would only need to work about five hours a day. The story was told with humour and related how the speaker laughed at his son and said: 'Good luck finding that place of employment.' But underlying the story was the idea that this generation has greater expectations of the workforce and their leaders. They expect greater transparency, opportunity and flexibility in the workplace.

The emerging generations and, indeed, all generations want more balance between competing priorities in their lives. Ask yourself the question: 'What would I do if I had 30 more minutes in each day?' The answers would range from family time to personal time and more time to get work done, highlighting the tension that exists between the competing priorities of our modern and busy lives.

What can be seen here is a common tension people face when it comes to 'work' and 'life', but work is too big a part of our lives to consider entirely separately to other aspects of our life even though these other aspects warrant time, attention and energy as well. This is why we don't so much use the term 'work/life balance' but 'work/life integration'. This latter term helps us see that work and life are ideally not in competition, but that our 'at work' life and our 'away from work' life are both key to our contributions, relationships and fulfilment. Work/life integration helps leaders view employees as holistic people with multiple needs and goals.

Just as workers bring their work home with them, so too do people bring their home to work. When leaders view employees as more than just employees, build trust with them and allow them to have better work/life integration, workers and therefore organisations have a better chance of thriving. It is unrealistic and unhealthy to silo our various roles in life.

The rise of the gig economy, a labour market characterised by the prevalence of short-term contracts or freelance work as opposed to permanent jobs, contributes to this. There is less differentiation between work life and out-of-work life, or your corporate job and your personal values. In response, organisations should ensure that prospective employees fit the role not just based on their competence, but also that their culture suits the organisations, and their character is a values match. When a worker feels that they fit the organisation, that their work/life integration is respected by the organisation and that they are a valued member of the team and that work is a place they belong, they have a greater chance of thriving.

Organisational leader Fay Calderone, an employment lawyer and partner at law firm Hall & Wilcox, said the term 'balance' has fallen from usage because it is too idealistic:

> When I started, I thought there needed to be a compartmentalisation of work in the one bucket and family and home life in the other, that you needed to maintain a level of professionalism at work and [have] boundaries. I found that personally challenging and very difficult to do. But as I developed in my profession, I realised that work is such a big part of our lives and we spend so much time in the workplace it's naive to assume people are not going to be their true selves and are not going to bring their authentic selves

and their strengths, weaknesses and challenges into the work environment.

I believe people have personal attributes and we need to harness those. We need to provide support for the challenges because what is challenging people outside of work is inevitably going to trickle into the workplace. I'm not suggesting we make excuses, but we also can't be uncompromising in the way we insist people perform. People are not robots. We have to take account of the human condition and to get the best out of people; we need to understand how people think, what motivates them and what their strengths are, what is going to make them flourish.

It's also naïve to expect that what's going to work for one person is going to work for another. So if we aren't taking into account people's individual attributes, we're more likely to build a one-size-fits-all solution to engagement and retention and to people's development. There's no way everyone can thrive under that.

Flexible working conditions are a normal and expected part of today's workplace and can help contribute to greater work/life integration and wellbeing. Three in five workers (60%) said flexible working hours are extremely or very important in their place of employment. Coming into the workforce at a time when the gig economy and contingent work are mainstream, the desire for flexibility is particularly true for the emerging Generation Zs.

Flexible workplace conditions are paramount for overall employee engagement and particularly for women in the workplace, who in Australia are more than twice as likely than men to be the primary carers (child, elder and disability carers). In the same way we are embracing technical skills and relational skills as we look to the future of work, so too will the next generation of female leaders increasingly seek to prioritise career advancement and family. Parents have a tremendous capacity to juggle various commitments, but to do so they need the right support in their workplaces such as flexibility and support when leaving the workforce.

Women are more likely than men to agree that not enough flexible working options (55% of women compared with 33% of men) and a lack of support for women exiting the workplace for family reasons (52% of women compared with 31% of men) are factors holding back Australian workplaces from achieving more women in senior leadership positions. While progress has been made with regard to gender equality in the workplace there is still a lot of room for improvement, including acceptance of the idea that both men and women need flexible working conditions to thrive.

One of the biggest barriers to flexibility in the workplace is a lack of trust that the work will be done when people are absent from the physical workplace and so not being observed. The Deloitte Millennials survey[5] found that 'a solid foundation of trust enables organisations to increasingly offer and operate flexible working arrangements'. This research explored different types of workplace flexibility and found that each has positive impacts. These include flexible time (employees choosing when they start/finish work), a flexible role (employees shaping their job role), flexible recruitment (offering different types of contracts) and flexible location (employees choosing to work from the office, home or other locations). These flexible working conditions are beneficial, not just for Millennials but across all generations as they seek to juggle multiple and competing priorities.

Increased levels of flexibility in all areas are positively correlated to greater personal benefit and loyalty and improved organisational performance. According to the Millennials survey:

Flexible working arrangements support greater productivity and employee engagement while enhancing their personal wellbeing, health, and happiness. Compared to those in 'low-flexibility' environments, those employed where flexible working is highly embedded are twice as likely to say it has a positive impact on organizational performance and personal wellbeing. Those in highly flexible workplaces are two-and-a-half times more likely than those in more restrictive organizations to say that flexible working practices have a positive impact on financial performance. This, if nothing else, should encourage businesses to further explore what might follow from having more flexible approaches to working arrangements.[6]

3. Varied job roles

A job that involves variety, enables workers to exercise their strengths and skills and provides opportunities for advancement is something many of us desire. More than half of workers (54%) say opportunities for advancement within the organisation are extremely or very important to them in their place of employment. This is even more pronounced in the emerging generation of workers, Generation Z, for whom three in five workers (63%) see opportunity for advancement in a job as extremely or very important. It is also one of their top three must-haves. Why do employees change jobs by moving to a new organisation when they may be able to change jobs within their existing organisation?

A job that doesn't lock workers into a narrow task but offers variety, flexibility and the chance of a promotion will enable people to grow. This is even more true for Generation Z, for whom change is like the air they breathe. They keep up with dynamic technologies, it is likely they will move homes more frequently than previous generations and they have come out of an education system that has offered greater subject choice than ever before. At this stage of their life variety is all they've known.

When workplaces, employers and leaders are intentional about the roles they design for the individual members of their teams, roles that have variety and are challenging and allow team members to make a difference, wellbeing is more likely to be achieved. A common misconception about wellbeing is that it merely refers to people being in a state of balance or rest. While consistency is important, wellbeing and thriving are about human flourishing or growing or developing in a healthy or vigorous way.

When workers are given a responsibility or a task outside of their comfort zone that stretches their capacity, almost all (94%) know that these types of tasks and experiences grow them. Two in five (41%) say they enjoy the process, while the majority (53%) say they don't enjoy the process but they know it grows them. Just 6% say they don't enjoy the process and don't find it helpful. These are positive findings that indicate that whether or not people like the feeling of being stretched, they know these sorts of opportunities are good for them because it helps them to grow. As leadership expert John Maxwell said: 'If we're growing, we're always going to be out of our comfort zone.' Growth, stretching in capacity and even the stress that accompanies this are not opposites to wellbeing. In fact, they contribute to flourishing. It is the responsibility of workplace leaders to identify opportunities for their teams to grow and stretch in their capacity, to offer training to help equip workers and give them variety in their roles.

When we asked the question about growing and stretching in capacity, men indicated they were more likely than women to enjoy the process and knew it stretched them (44% of men compared to 36% of women). Inversely, women were more likely than men to agree that, while they didn't always enjoy the process, they knew being given a responsibility or task outside of their comfort zone that stretched their capacity grew them (60% of women agreed compared to 49% of men).

Ashley: This finding tells me we need courageous leaders who will step up and provide opportunities for training and advancement and ensure that their team members have job variety, particularly among the female team members in the workplace. I have read a number of books and articles on the topic of typical gender behaviour. Many studies (including the one we conducted) told me that women are not stepping up as much as men for opportunities where they do not feel qualified or confident enough. This needs to change if we want wellbeing to ensue in our teams, workplaces and society. Women need to speak up, to be given seats at the table and have opportunities to grow. Leaders should be aware of these differences, that men often enjoy the process of being stretched more than women and so are likely to put their hands up first.

> Women need these opportunities as well, and leaders need to be aware of it.

When workers have job variety, are challenged in their role and are growing they are less likely to leave an organisation for an opportunity elsewhere. There will always be lower retention rates among younger staff compared to older generations, but retention can be improved through: accessibility, by taking the mystery out of how decisions are made; variety, by giving junior staff greater responsibility or better roles in their work (conducting exit interviews, giving presentations, organising staff events); and entrusting younger staff members to give something a go.

Another tip: understand the revolving door. If people leave for a new job or further study, keep in touch – they may want to return later. This is particularly true for the emerging Generation Zs, who don't view leaving an organisation as an act of disloyalty but a simple life change and see no problem with returning should circumstances change.

4. Leadership style

When it comes to workplace factors, there are few elements that have a bigger impact on the wellbeing of individuals and teams than leadership. The style with which leaders and managers lead in workplaces has a direct impact on workers' ability to thrive. Leadership was covered in more detail in Chapter 7.

Leadership has a huge impact on retention of workers. In a survey we conducted with Reventure of employed Australians, almost half (46%) of those who planned on looking for a new job within the next two years said that the poor leadership at their workplace was the most stressful part of their job. This was much more likely among those intending to look for a new job in the next two years (46%) than it was among those who did not plan on looking for a new job in the next two years (25%).[7]

Those planning on leaving were also more likely to feel the negative culture in their workplace (42%) compared to those not planning on leaving (25%). Similarly, those planning on leaving were more likely to indicate their boss lacked clear vision and direction (39% of those who planned to leave agreed with this, compared with 8% of those who did not plan to leave). Perhaps the most severe finding of all was that more than a third (36%) of those who planned on looking for a new job in the next two years were actively looking to leave the organisation because of the leader directly above them.[8]

The findings are clear: unless direct supervisors and the leadership hierarchy manage in an inclusive, participative way and demonstrate people skills and not just technical skills, retention declines. Leadership is a big deal.

In our recent worker survey, almost three in five (58%) said that inspiring and accessible leadership was extremely or very important to them in their place of employment. Simon Sinek said: 'We are drawn to leaders and organisations that are good at communicating what they believe. Their ability to make us feel like we belong, to make us feel special, safe and not alone is part of what gives them the ability to inspire us.'

Before we can manage and lead we must be able to understand and connect. Workers are now working in a very different environment to that of the past. Their expectations of a leader, attitudes to the job and preferred styles of work have all been shaped by their times. Workplaces are diverse: generationally and culturally and from a gender perspective. If leaders hope to lead thriving teams they will need to understand their teams, and the first part of better understanding is to listen more.

As social researchers who study human behaviour we are constantly surveying specific communities and speaking to people in focus groups and in-depth interviews about a number of topics. This is the value of research, that it tests hypotheses by listening to individuals, groups, communities and societies. Leaders who make decisions after speaking with and listening to those they are leading – whether it be their teams or colleagues, clients or stakeholders – rather than on assumptions or gut feel are informed leaders who gain the respect and trust of their teams. It can be difficult to prioritise in a culture of busyness and 'just get it done', but if we want to improve interpersonal relationships and get better results we need to listen to the perspectives of those in our communities.

Stephen Covey in his book *The 7 Habits of Highly Effective People* listed as one of his habits: *seek first to understand then to be understood.* He wrote: 'Most leaders and managers could dramatically improve organizational productivity and their own effectiveness if they just truly valued listening to others more.'[9]

Former police commissioner Andrew Scipione spoke about the importance of being a leader who listens, who cares about staff and who builds trust and respect among their team. He said:

> A lot of leadership practice comes down to listening to those who you serve and understanding them. My role was to serve two specific groups. One, most importantly, was the community. The second, the police force, the men and the women of the organisation. When I became commissioner, I said the first thing we're going to do is go back and talk to the people who we serve. So we ran focus groups. I sat behind the smoked glass on many occasions and just watched and listened. Then we then had to go back and talk to our people. I would get large groups together and talk with them. And we said, 'We're here, as an organisation, for one reason: and that's to serve the community that we protect.'
>
> So we started talking to them about customer service. And many said, 'Hang on, our customers are criminals.' We had to get them to refocus because really, in terms of overall numbers, 80% of the community are on your side; they're not the criminals. So let's start focusing on the 80% who really we never have focused on before. They struggled with that until we said it means dealing with every person that comes into the station and talks to you and asks for help, like it was your

mother, or your sister, or your wife, or your daughter or your uncle. How would you want them to be treated? If they were treated poorly you'd be complaining tomorrow and rightly so. These people have a right to be treated well.

We wanted the community to come to us. The only way you will ever get people to trust you is if you have a relationship, and for me it was talking to the community often. For any organisation, the destiny is shaped by the people who are the stewards, who carry the brand.

The ability to listen is a key characteristic of the collaborative leadership style, which is the preferred leadership style of workers. Two in five workers (40%) said they preferred a collaborative leadership style, a highly participative style with the leader leading by example and from within the group and the team collaborating to deliver the outcomes. Almost two in five (38%) preferred a co-ordinated leadership style, which is still an interactive approach with the leader giving some direction and the team making contributions.

Very few (16%) opted for the more traditional hierarchical leadership style, a structured environment with the leader in control and with some limited interaction. Even fewer (6%) selected the autocratic style, with the leader in an authoritarian position and the staff following directions.

Overall, workers prefer collaborative leaders who value communication and create an environment of involvement and respect for staff. Their leadership style is one that is consensus rather than command, participative rather than autocratic and more flexible and organic than structured and hierarchical.

Global Leadership consultants Oxford Leadership define collaborative leadership as:

The process of engaging collective intelligence to deliver results across organisational boundaries. It's grounded in a belief that all of us together can be smarter, more creative, and more competent than any of us alone, especially when it comes to addressing the kinds of novel, complex, and multi-faceted problems that organisations face today. It calls on leaders to use the power of influence rather than positional authority to engage and align people, focus their teams, sustain momentum, and perform. Success depends on creating an environment of trust, mutual respect, and shared aspiration in which all can contribute fully and openly to achieving collective goals. Leaders must thus focus on relationships as well as results, and the medium through which they operate is high-quality conversation.[10]

Collaborative leadership styles that encourage collective intelligence, decision making and contributions from team members create environments where all workers can contribute fully and openly to achieving the collective goals. The leader's key role is not to single-handedly achieve the outcome, but to shape the environment so that team success is inevitable. The leader therefore is one who knows the way, prepares the way and resources the way.

In *The Five Dysfunctions of a Team*, Patrick Lencioni describes the many pitfalls that teams face as they seek to grow together. After exploring the fundamental causes of organisational politics and team failure, he identified the following five dysfunctions:

- ❖ the absence of trust: the fear of being vulnerable with team members prevents the building of trust within a team

- ❖ fear of conflict: the desire to preserve artificial harmony stifles the occurrence of productive, ideological conflict

- ❖ lack of commitment: the lack of clarity or buy-in prevents team members from making decisions they will stick to

- ❖ avoidance of accountability: the need to avoid interpersonal discomfort prevents team members from holding one another accountable for behaviour and performance

❖ inattention to results: the pursuit of individual goals and personal status erodes the focus on collective success.[11]

Leaders who encourage, facilitate and create opportunities for collaboration in their workplaces help to overcome some of these common dysfunctions. In particular, collaborative leaders help their teams to commit to the vision and purpose, to ideas and decisions. When workers commit, have buy-in and feel part of the process and that their contributions are heard and valued they can thrive.

The ability to overcome these dysfunctions in organisations can be difficult, yet it can be done through collaborative leadership. Collaborative leaders are accessible leaders. Gone are the days when it was accepted that the leader would sit in an ivory tower, in closed-off offices on the top floor and out of touch with the rest of their organisation. Collaborative leaders need to be accessible and lead from within their teams. Positively, almost three in five workers we surveyed (58%) strongly or somewhat agreed that their workplace leader was accessible.

We asked Thankyou's co-founder Daniel Flynn what his most important leadership advice would be. His answer? Time: 'Time with your direct reports. Time with your wider team. This answer isn't because I've nailed that – but because I haven't. I've seen the damage lack of time has on the vision you are leading and the disconnects that can be created. Time to take people on the journey, time to celebrate the wins, time to cry and laugh together and remind yourselves of where you are going. There is no substitute. Time is your greatest asset and your team needs part of your greatest asset, not just what you have left over at the end of all the work you are trying to achieve.'

Ashley: At a recent conference on leadership, one of the speakers told the story of a prominent leader they knew whose executive assistant was instructed not to schedule any meetings before 9.15 am. Why? Because this leader made it a priority to dedicate the first 45 minutes of their day to speaking with the employees, looking them in the eye, connecting and giving their time to their team. This is the sign of a great leader, someone who is accessible to the people they lead. In an ever-increasingly busy world, when people dedicate and give their greatest asset — their time — it shows what, or rather who, they value.

The ideal leader gives public affirmation through pats on the back, both figurative and literal. They remember names and the interests of their staff, and create an emotionally safe, friendly, collegial environment where people feel free to contribute ideas. This is particularly important for our emerging Generation Z workers, who have a strong relationship ethic and who are collaborative learners. Generation Z enjoy working in teams and thrive in relaxed, consensus-driven groups.

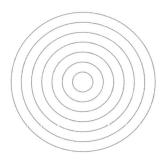

'The leader's key role is not to single-handedly achieve the outcome, but to shape the environment so that team success is inevitable. The leader therefore is one who knows the way, prepares the way and resources the way.'

– McCRINDLE

5. Training

Training, upskilling and investing in people's professional and personal development first and foremost benefits the individual worker. Training also shows the individual that the workplace values them and cares about their growth and development. Second, training benefits the workplace as the worker applies their newfound skills to their work, at the same time upskilling and retraining other team members. This transfer of knowledge benefits both the team and the organisation.

Around half of workers (48%) said that professional development (courses and training) were extremely or very important to them. This was even higher among Generation Z (52%) and Generation Y (57%), compared with Generation X (43%) and the Baby Boomers (38%). More remarkable than this was that training is more than a tool for productivity; it is a tool for retention. When invested in by their employer, workers are motivated to stay longer.

In our consulting work with organisations regarding attracting, retaining and training top talent, we have noticed an element of fear some leaders have of investing in training their team members. This is largely due to the fact that turnover is so high, with the average tenure in one role currently being just two years and eight months.

> **Ashley:** I spoke at a conference about the importance of investing in training staff, particularly those in the younger generations, as a key attraction and particularly a retention strategy. It's the idea that training leads to retaining. At the end, an attendee spoke about how they held the common perspective of: 'What's the point in training someone and having them go?' Another quickly responded: 'What if you *don't* train them and they stay?' Everyone in the audience was impacted by the clever use of these words to shift the perspective of how to view training as an investment and retention strategy.

Ensuring that our teams are adequately trained not only makes them better prepared for their jobs, it provides an opportunity for leaders to show their employees they care about them as people beyond just being workers who need to deliver outputs or meet certain targets and KPIs. When leaders approach employees and offer them the opportunity to attend a training course or upskill initiative, it shows that the leadership and the organisation are investing in them and they want to see them thrive.

In our worker survey, less than half of employees (49%) agreed that they felt invested in as a worker. This had one of the lowest percentages of agreement from the 19 statements we tested. Positively, 59% of workers strongly or somewhat agreed that the leaders in their workplace ensured people had the skills, expertise and resources to do the job.

Training leads to retaining, shows workers leaders care about them and improves work wellbeing. As Sir Richard Branson said: 'Train people well enough so they can leave. Treat them well enough so they don't want to.'

Training is a necessary part of all workers' lives, regardless of where you sit in an organisational hierarchy or how many years you've been working. Continually investing in training and upskilling is an essential way to futureproof yourself in times of change.

Clearly ongoing training is important for emerging generations, who are beginning their working life as the fourth industrial revolution gets underway. Generation Z accept the mantra of lifelong education; after all, many of them are working in industries and with technologies that didn't even exist when they were beginning high school such as drone operators, data designers and robotics technicians. A widely sourced World Economic Forum report predicts that 65% of children entering primary school today will ultimately end up working in completely new job types that don't yet exist.[12] The world of work is undergoing significant transformations.

However, it's not just the emerging generations who need to prepare for an uncertain future of work with multiple jobs and careers. The trends of longevity (people living longer and working later in life), automation (where technology will replace current functions and jobs currently held by human beings), globalisation (the ability to outsource work) and less predictable career paths are all aiding the fact that we will all, regardless of age or life stage, need to be lifelong learners, plugging back into education to upskill and retrain regularly.

According to an AlphaBeta report for Google Australia, 'Today, more than 80% of the time we spend in education and training occurs before the age of 21. But the idea that a post-secondary qualification will set us up for life is no longer a reality. In the future, workers will not be able to rely solely on what they learned as a teenager. To remain employable, workers will need to make a habit of refreshing existing skills and adding new ones throughout their career.'[13]

The report also says that 'the most valuable skills will be distinctively human characteristics', and that: 'In particular, complex and context-dependent human characteristics like empathy or leadership are challenging to translate into a language that a machine can understand … tasks that require tacit capabilities – ideas and wisdom that are highly subjective, context-specific, and related to intuition and personal experience – are much more difficult to codify for machines.'

The future of work will include jobs suited to technologically savvy young people such as quantum computing, biometric programming and AI technicians. However, new jobs such as wellbeing managers, office concierges, life simplifiers and urban farmers are also emerging and are roles where experience and people skills favour repositioning workers and not just new, younger workers.

Many organisations and leaders focus on ensuring their teams are equipped with technical skills that often are relevant only for a current job. While these skills are important to a certain extent, people skills are both transferable and lifelong and are in demand in more machine-assisted workplaces.

To future proof our teams we need to develop people skills, not just technical skills.

'Train people well enough so they can leave. Treat them well enough so they don't want to.'

– SIR RICHARD BRANSON

In our worker survey we asked the question: '*If you had the opportunity to attend a company-provided or paid for training session, what would be your preferred type of training?*' We gave four options: operational skills (job specific e.g. software, tool and technique training); technical skills (e.g. sales training, system management, client liaison); people skills (e.g. leadership training, managing a team, collaboration); and communication skills (e.g. presentation skills, public speaking).

When broken down by generation, Generation Z are the most likely to prefer training in the areas of soft skills (62%) compared with Generation Y (45%), Generation X (37%) or the Baby Boomers (36%). The older a worker is the less likely they are to prefer training in the area of soft skills and the more likely they are to prefer training in the area of hard skills. However Generation Z have as their first preference people skills. Females are also more likely than males to prefer training in soft skills (49% of females compared to 38% of males).

Training doesn't have to take place outside the office or offsite as long as it is engaging. On-the-job coaching/mentoring as well as in-house or outsourced training courses can all be effective ways of investing in training staff and work well for the emerging generations. This is due in part to their learning styles (kinaesthetic and visual rather than literate and procedural) as well as their learning motivations (collaborative, interactive and fun!).

In the span of a generation or so we have transitioned from lifelong careers to lifelong learning. The key to remaining relevant in changing times is ongoing training, which will keep employees effective in their current job and employable for their future careers which, after all, may be just a few years away. It is important that re-skillers (those who are changing jobs), upskillers (those refreshing their skills) and future workers all invest in training.

Founder and CEO of digital strategy agency ntegrity, Richenda Vermeulen, spoke at length about how to attract, recruit and retain top talent in a competitive environment where turnover is high: 'What's been key to attracting the right people and keeping them is we've just found people that share our purpose. So often when we're hiring, they have read through our website or seen a speaking event and said: "That sounds like me." We've gone through our own processes to really understand what makes the team that has worked tick and how we can continue to attract more people like that.'

Richenda also shared how her team is focused on both growth for their clients and growth for their team:

> We overestimate salary. Salary is definitely important; people want to be paid fairly and know that there's a trajectory. But what I've found to be more important is having a conversation with someone about their growth and their growth plans, and not being so close minded about thinking that it has to be focused on work. So by being able to say: what are you interested in in the next five years, whether that's your next job, whether that's picking up a skillset, whether that's wanting to become a parent. Not being so scared to talk about things outside of work.
>
> Say for example I want half a day a week to create art but I don't want to quit my job and become an artist, staff have to feel that there's no retribution in sharing those things. The more we can see where someone can grow, what they want to do in their life and in their work, the longer we're going to retain them.

Every quarter her staff members meet with a coach to discuss their business and professional goals. Interestingly, Richenda said they also discuss personal goals:

> It is totally optional, but we want people to have a space to talk about their personal goals and use this as an accountability point. So for some people they might say run a marathon. For someone else it might be write a blog post. For me it's getting more sleep, which is going well this year! And some staff, I can really see if they haven't had their session as they're quite disorientated.
>
> Our team also enjoy getting offsite and having time together for our quarterly strategy day. Everyone works really hard in the morning on the business, and more lightly on themselves in the

afternoon. And then we have a big dinner and we might do an activity, or we might have breakfast together the next day.

I think a lot of the time people talk about company retreats with cynicism, which I used to do before running them as well. Because you can talk about all these things, but what does it actually translate into? But we take that investment really seriously. We're up to our 20th strategy day now, and it's definitely the secret sauce to company growth. It keeps us focused on what we need to be doing.

Workplace leaders can enhance employee wellbeing by focusing on the elements of workplace culture, work/life integration, leadership, training and job variety. In our survey of workers we asked about the impact of different workplace elements on the attitude and culture of workers, with leadership, internal relationships and the work environment all having a significant impact.

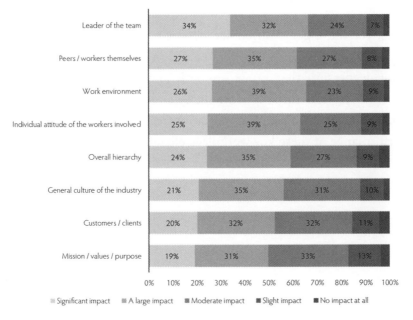

What type of impact does the following have on the attitude and culture of workers?

In this survey we also tested a number of workplace areas as to what the priority of these elements are in the workplace (expectation), but also how workplaces are performing in these areas (reality).

	PRIORITY	PERFORMANCE	DIFFERENCE
Workplace flexibility	58%	43%	15%
Purpose and meaning (I know why I am here)	58%	45%	13%
Investment in my professional development	55%	38%	17%
Engaging and enlarging leadership that grows my strength and capacity	54%	38%	16%
A social environment that provides non-monetary rewards	47%	35%	12%
Creating a community of strong social connections	46%	38%	8%

For workers, the biggest priority is workplace flexibility and purpose and meaning, yet the biggest difference between priority and performance is in the areas of investing in professional development and engaging and enlarging leadership that grows strength and capacity. If organisational leaders want to lead thriving workplaces and employees, then a strategy needs to be in place to close the expectation/reality gap between the priority and performance of these key workplace elements.

CHAPTER 10

CONCLUSION

There is always a temptation for businesses to succumb to the worst tenets of postmodern capitalism with its singular focus on shareholder returns decoupled from a moral compass. However, traditional capitalism, like most businesses have at their core, contains the virtues of value creation, shared ownership, thrift, savings and investment and a commitment to the common good. The constitutions of many of our largest companies and financial institutions give evidence of these values and the intent behind their incorporation. Australia's central bank, the Reserve Bank of Australia, sets out in its 1959 charter its three purposes in the exercise of its powers. In addition to the goal of stability of the currency and maintenance of full employment is the broader wellbeing goal 'the economic prosperity and welfare of the people of Australia'.

We find this same aspiration at the heart of many business leaders today. While modern employment and its compensation can feed covetousness and greed, our research shows that many leaders see they have a bigger purpose, which is to enhance the wellbeing of their teams, organisation and community. This is in unison with the emerging generations, who similarly have a more enlightened definition of success. For many entering the workplace, success is not just defined financially but holistically. 'Am

I doing what I love?', 'Is it meaningful?', 'Am I contributing to a better world?' and 'Are we a part of something bigger than ourselves?'

These are interesting times in which to lead and facilitate work wellbeing.

Only occasionally in history do massive demographic shifts combine with rapid social change and huge generational transitions and ongoing technology trends, so that within the span of a decade society altogether alters. We are now living in one such transformative decade. From the gig economy to remote working and digital disruption, all these shifts are impacting how, when and where people work. The forced adoption of working from home that we all experienced through COVID-19 highlighted that work wellbeing was not dependent on a place. The fact that globally the workplace became one's home did not diminish the role of employers to facilitate team wellbeing; rather, it heightened it.

In our research, workers have acknowledged that the number one trend that will have the most significant impact is the mental health and stress of workers (above demographic trends, the physical work space and where work will be done, sectors disappearing, computerisation of robotics, global workforce flows and the gig economy). As the distinction between home and work continues to blur and as many workers seek to find greater balance for the competing priorities in their lives, the workplace can either help to pile up the burdens of overwork, stress, burnout and a focus on productivity or it can help to alleviate some of these burdens by prioritising people and their health and wellbeing above key performance indicators and key vehicles of productivity.

Amid the challenges of COVID-19, so much of what we took for granted as 'normal' came to an end. Whether supermarkets would have the groceries we needed, whether going for a drive was a valid reason to be out, how we would even get our hair cut began to occupy our thoughts. However, work remained a pleasant constant. In the midst of all this change the need for work, and the role, purpose and value it brings to people's lives beyond just the financial reward, continues to remain relevant. Work that is good for us, that aligns to a greater purpose and enables us to contribute is key to human flourishing and wellbeing.

As these chapters have shown, the best leaders are those who understand the times and can engage effectively with each new generation of team members, but these leaders also need to remember the foundations on which their organisation was built and be the custodians of those values and foundational purposes. They lean back even while they move forward. The strength of an organisation comes from its stories and traditions, but the future of an organisation rests in its relevance and innovation.

This has come up time and time again in our extensive research of workers. We asked the question: 'Other than to get paid, how important is your work in contributing to the following areas?'

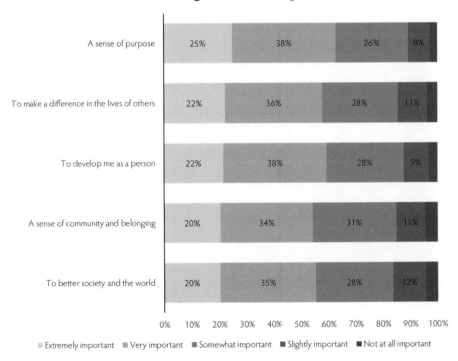

Other than to get paid, how important is your work in contributing to the following areas?

Work is considered extremely or very important to:

❖ developing a sense of purpose (63%)

❖ developing as a person (59%)

❖ making a difference in the lives of others (58%)

❖ bettering society and the world (55%)

❖ contributing to a sense of community and belonging (54%)

This presents a great opportunity for the workplace to help in these important areas of personal growth and fulfilment.

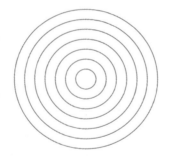

'The strength of an organisation comes from its stories and traditions, but the future of an organisation rests in its relevance and innovation.'

– McCRINDLE

There are certainly some harsh realities in today's business world. Business leaders are required to output more in less time and with less cost to the organisation, but if people are an organisation's greatest asset then organisational leaders who prioritise the wellbeing of their teams, focus on their growth and development, challenge them and encourage and equip them to grow will help their organisations to flourish and thrive.

If leaders want to attract talent, retain them for longer and ensure they are brand promotors and organisational advocates, employers and workplace leaders need to help ensure their workers can function at their greatest capacity and utilise their unique strengths.

The key role of a leader is to influence, motivate and lead people to an organisational outcome and to deliver on its key objectives. Leaders who lead collaboratively, who are accessible to their teams and who prioritise the people they lead and have a long-term focus have a better chance of leading transformative rather than transactional workplace cultures. Organisations that prioritise the wellbeing of their teams, take the time to listen and understand the changing composition of their workforce as well as observe, respond and innovate in response to a changing world will thrive in the years to come.

As many elements of our global, political and social context remain unstable, workplace leaders have a unique opportunity before them to transform the workplace and team members and the outputs they deliver, and to be a positive force for good. Workplaces that are sustainable and engaging, prioritise the health and wellbeing of their teams and create an engaging workplace culture, purpose and impact are better placed to lead thriving teams and therefore thriving organisations.

Not only does prioritising wellbeing help individuals and workers to thrive, it translates to higher performance and productivity for the organisation. This means that work wellbeing is critical not only for individual flourishing and thriving, but for organisational and societal flourishing as well.

J.R.R. Tolkien, well-known as the author of *The Hobbit* and *The Lord of the Rings* trilogy, wrote a little, lesser-known short story: Leaf by Niggle. Niggle was an artist with a vision to paint a glorious mural of a majestic tree in the public square. Due to his perfectionist tendencies he could never quite get the tree, or even small parts of it, to look like the vision he had for it. As indicated by his name he was plagued by frustrations, interruptions and illnesses, and despite his commitment and hard work he died before he had got much finished beyond one stunning leaf. As he was carried over into the afterlife and guided to his eternal domain he stopped when he saw a tree, his tree, just as he'd imagined it but there: full, real, perfect. And there he stood, staring, clapping in delight and exclaiming 'There is a tree!'

It is a great reminder that our work matters even though it may not match our expectation or vision, because, ultimately, the values and purpose of what we do exist in full. One's work as a lawyer seeking justice matters because justice exists. One's work as a community worker matters because altruism, genuine care and authenticity exist. There is a tree. And so it is with our work: it matters, and in an ultimate sense it exists in fullness and is of timeless worth.

Leaders create ripples of impact: 'I alone
cannot change the world, but I can cast a stone
across the waters to create many ripples.'

- SAINT TERESA OF CALCUTTA

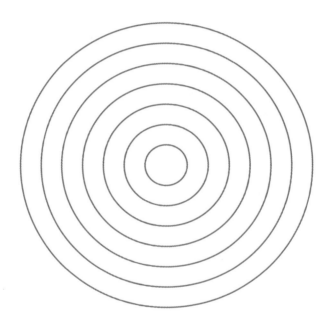

Leaders facilitate growth in people: 'Like the growth rings of a tree,
our lives occasionally experience seasons of extraordinary flourishing.
We have found three catalysts for such growth: significant adversity,
extreme dissatisfaction, or exposure to an exceptional leader.'

- McCRINDLE

OVERVIEW
OF RESEARCH
METHODOLOGIES

THE WORKER SURVEYS

Two surveys were conducted for the purpose of this book.[1]

The first was conducted by McCrindle Research in February 2019 and was based on a nationwide study of 1,160 respondents. To qualify for this survey, respondents had to be between the ages of 18 and 65 and be employed either full time, part time or on a casual basis or be self-employed.

The second was conducted by McCrindle Research in June 2019 and was based on a nationwide study of 1,001 respondents. To qualify for this survey, respondents had to be between the ages of 18 and 65 and employed either full time, part time or on a casual basis or be self-employed.

THE FUTURE OF EDUCATION REPORT

The Future of Education report conducted by McCrindle Research[2] collates both quantitative and qualitative data. Quantitative data was collected through an online survey, while qualitative data was gathered through two focus groups and five in-depth interviews.

Online survey

The survey of Generation Y and Generation X parents was conducted in field in July 2019. It was completed by a sample of 447 Generation Y parents and 555 Generation X parents, providing a total sample of 1,002 Australian parents.

Focus groups

Two focus groups with Generation Y teachers were conducted in July 2019 (with seven participants) and August 2019 (with seven participants).[3]

THE REGRETS SURVEY

This study was conducted by McCrindle Research in November 2019 and was based on a nationwide study of 1,008 respondents.

FAITH AND BELIEF REPORT

This research employed qualitative and quantitative methods to explore Australian perceptions and attitudes towards faith and spirituality. These methods included a nationally representative survey of Australians, a series of focus groups and analysis of data from the Australian Bureau of Statistics.[4]

REMOTE WORKING SURVEY

This study was conducted by McCrindle Research in April 2013 and was based on a nationwide study of 580 respondents.

WORKPLACE WELLBEING REPORT

The workplace wellbeing report is a collation of data gained through a quantitative survey conducted through an online panel. The survey was in field in April 2017 and consisted of a nationally representative survey of 1,005 Australian employed adults aged between 18 and 65 years.[5]

PRECARIOUS WORK INSIGHTS REPORT

The precarious work insights report is a collation of data gained through a quantitative survey conducted through an online panel. The survey was in field from 23 April to 3 May 2018 and consisted of a nationally representative survey of 1,007 Australian employed adults aged between 18 and 65 years.[6]

WORKPLACE LONELINESS REPORT

The workplace loneliness report is the collation of data obtained through a quantitative survey conducted with an online panel. The survey was in field from 15 March to 21 March 2019 and was completed by a nationally representative sample of 1,010 employed Australians aged between 18 and 65 years.[7]

AUSTRALIANS AMIDST COVID-19 REPORT

This research was conducted by McCrindle in conjunction with our panel partner Cint. The report is based on an online survey deployed to a nationally representative sample of 1,015 Australians. Data was collected between 19 and 23 March 2020.

NOTES

Introduction

[1] Black Dog Institute, Youth mental health report: Youth Survey 2012-16, bit.ly/2VC6fg4.

[2] F.M. Gore, P.J. Bloem, G.C. Patton, J. Ferguson, V. Joseph, C. Coffey, S.M. Sawyer and C.D. Mathers, 'Global burden of disease in young people aged 10–24 years: a systematic analysis', *The Lancet*, vol. 377, issue 9783, 18 June 2011, pp. 2093-2102.

[3] McCrindle, Education Future Report, 2019, https://mccrindle.com.au/insights/publications/reports-and-summaries/education-future-report-2016/.

[4] ibid.

[5] Stephen Harris blog, 2020, http://stephenharris.me/profile.

[6] World Health Organization, Mental Health: strengthening our response, 30 March 2018, https://www.who.int/news-room/fact-sheets/detail/mental-health-strengthening-our-response.

[7] World Health Organization, Constitution, 7 April 1948, https://www.who.int/about/who-we-are/constitution.

[8] Victoria state government Better Health Channel, Wellbeing, https://www.betterhealth.vic.gov.au/health/healthyliving/wellbeing.

[9] Safe Work Australia, 'News', February 2020, https://www.safeworkaustralia.gov.au/media-centre/news/latest-reports-whs-and-workers-compensation-australia-and-new-zealand-now.

Chapter 1: What is work wellbeing?

[1] Merriam-Webster, Breaking Bread with 'Companion', 2020, https://www.merriam-webster.com/words-at-play/history-of-word-companion.

[2] Reventure, A Future that Works, The Workplace Well-being Report, November 2017, http://www.afuturethatworks.org.au/reports.

3 Martin E.P. Seligman, *Flourish: A visionary new understanding of happiness and well-being*, Simon and Schuster, 2011.

4 ibid.

5 ibid.

6 NEF Consulting, Wellbeing at Work: a review of the literature, February 2014.

Chapter 2: Diversity in the workplace

1 World Economic Forum, The Future of Jobs: Employment, Skills and Workforce Strategy for the Fourth Industrial Revolution, January 2016.

2 McKinsey & Company, *Women in the Workplace*, October 2018, https://www.mckinsey.com/featured-insights/gender-equality/women-in-the-workplace-2018.

3 ibid.

4 Gallup, Three Requirements of a Diverse and Inclusive Culture – and Why They Matter for Your Organization, 2018, https://www.gallup.com/workplace/242108/diversity-inclusion-perspective-paper.aspx.

5 Australian government, Workplace Gender Equality Agency, Gender workplace statistics at a glance, 2019, https://www.wgea.gov.au/data/fact-sheets/gender-workplace-statistics-at-a-glance-2018-19.

6 Arianna Huffington, *Thrive: The Third Metric to Redefining Success and Creating a Life of Well-Being, Wisdom, and Wonder*, Harmony, 2014.

7 Australian government, Australian Institute of Health and Welfare, Older Australia at a glance, 10 September 2018, https://www.aihw.gov.au/reports/older-people/older-australia-at-a-glance/contents/summary.

8 Stephen Covey, *The 7 Habits of Highly Effective People: Powerful lessons in personal change*, Free Press, 2004.

9 Australian Bureau of Statistics, Births, Australia, 2017: Australian women are now having children older than ever, 11 December 2018, cat. 3301.0.

10 Mark McCrindle, *The ABC of XYZ: Understanding the Global Generations*, UNSW Press, 2009.

11 Deloitte, The evolution of work: New realities facing today's leaders, 2018, https://www2.deloitte.com/tr/en/pages/human-capital/articles/the-evolution-of-work.html.

12 Daniel Flynn, *Chapter One: You have the power to change stuff*, The Messenger Group, 2016.

13 United States Census Bureau and the Migration Observatory at the University of Oxford.

14 Australian Bureau of Statistics, Counts of Australian Businesses, including Entries and Exits: Key Statistics, June 2014 to June 2018, cat. 8165.0.

15 Reventure, A Future that Works, Workplace Loneliness, 2019, http://www.afuturethatworks.org.au/reports.

[16] Triple J, What's Up in Your World, 2018, https://www.abc.net.au/triplej/programs/hack/whats-up-in-your-world-the-census-for-young-people/10051266.

[17] Reventure, A Future that Works, Precarious Work Insights, 2018, http://www.afuturethatworks.org.au/reports.

[18] Reventure, A Future that Works, Workplace Loneliness, 2019, http://www.afuturethatworks.org.au/reports.

[19] Deloitte, The 2017 Deloitte Millennials Survey, 2017, bit.ly/ 2B1eVml.

Chapter 3: Why work wellbeing must be the key issue

[1] World Health Organization, Five Well-being Index (WHO-5), 2018, https://www.corc.uk.net/outcome-experience-measures/the-world-health-organisation-five-well-being-index-who-5/.

[2] Arianna Huffington, *Thrive*, Harmony, 2014.

[3] World Health Organization, Burn-out an 'occupational phenomenon': International Classification of Diseases, 28 May 2019, https://www.who.int/mental_health/evidence/burn-out/en/.

[4] Arianna Huffington, *Thrive*, Harmony, 2014.

[5] ibid.

[6] Reventure, A Future that Works, Workplace Loneliness, 2019, http://www.afuturethatworks.org.au/reports.

Chapter 4: Barriers to work wellbeing

[1] TopResume, Signs You're in a Toxic Work Environment – and How to Handle It, 2020, https://www.topresume.com/career-advice/how-to-handle-toxic-work-environment.

[2] David Gillespie, *Taming Toxic People: The science of identifying & dealing with psychopaths at work & at home*, Macmillan Australia, 2017.

[3] Clint Jasper, Corporate psychopath rates 'similar to prison population', https://www.abc.net.au/news/2016-09-13/tool-to-screen-for-psychopaths/7839854.

[4] Reventure, A Future that Works, Snapshot of the Australian Workplace, 2018, bit/ly/35uIOcL.

[5] Patrick Lencioni, *The Five Dysfunctions of a Team: A leadership fable*, Jossey-Bass, 2002.

[6] ibid.

Chapter 5: Pillars of work wellbeing

[1] Martin E.P. Seligman, *Flourish*, Simon and Schuster, 2011.

[2] Matthew Walker, *Why We Sleep: Unlocking the power of sleep and dreams*, Scribner, 2017.

[3] Arianna Huffington, *Thrive*, Harmony, 2014.

[4] World Health Organization, Mental health: a state of well-being, https://www.who.int/about/who-we-are/constitution.

[5] Martin E.P. Seligman, *Flourish*, Simon and Schuster, 2011.

[6] ibid.

[7] Michelle McQuaid and Dr Peggy Kern, *Your Wellbeing Blueprint: Feeling good and doing well at work*, Michelle McQuaid Pty Limited, 2017.

[8] Reventure, A Future that Works, Workplace Loneliness, 2019, http://www.afuturethatworks.org.au/reports.

[9] ibid.

[10] ibid.

[11] Martin E.P. Seligman, *Flourish*, Simon and Schuster, 2011.

[12] Daniel Flynn, *Chapter One*, The Messenger Group, 2016.

[13] Martin E.P. Seligman, *Flourish*, Simon and Schuster, 2011.

[14] Reventure, A Future that Works, Precarious Work Insights, 2018, http://www.afuturethatworks.org.au/reports.

Chapter 6: How to foster work wellbeing

[1] Simon Sinek, Start with Why: How great leaders inspire everyone to take action, Portfolio, 2009.

[2] ibid.

[3] ERC, Workplace Culture: What It Is, Why It Matters, and How to Define It, 1 February 2019, https://www.yourerc.com/blog/post/workplace-culture-what-it-is-why-it-matters-how-to-define-it.

[4] Simon Sinek, *Start with Why*, Portfolio, 2011.

[5] Martin E.P. Seligman, *Flourish*, Simon and Schuster, 2011.

[6] Daniel Coyle, *The Culture Code: The secrets of highly successful groups*, Bantam, 2016.

[7] Simon Sinek, *Start with Why*, Portfolio, 2011.

[8] Medallia, Net Promoter Score, 2020, https://www.medallia.com/net-promoter-score/.

[9] Patrick Lencioni, *The 5 Dysfunctions of a Team*, Jossey-Bass, 2002.

[10] Simon Sinek, *Start with Why*, Portfolio, 2011.

[11] ibid.

[12] ibid.

[13] Lambert Deckers, *Motivation: Biological, Psychological, and Environmental*, Routledge Press, 2018.

[14] Martin Seligman, *Flourish*, Simon and Schuster, 2011.

[15] The Garis Group, 'My Biggest Mistake': Entrepreneurs Reveal Where They Went, Wrong, 22 July 2016, https://www.garis.com.au/biggest-mistake-entrepreneurs-reveal-went-wrong/.

Chapter 7: Leading teams in changing times

[1] Stephen Covey, *The 7 Habits of Highly Effective People: Powerful lessons in personal change*, Free Press, 2004.

[2] Gallup, Gallup's Approach to Culture: Building a culture that drives performance, 2018, https://www.gallup.com/workplace/232682/culture-paper-2018.aspx.

[3] Daniel Coyle, *The Culture Code*, Bantam, 2016.

[4] Jim Collins, *Good to Great: Why Some Companies Make the Leap . . . and Others Don't*, HarperBusiness, 2001.

[5] AlphaBeta for Google Australia, Future Skills: The rise of machines will drive a need for more lifelong learning in Australia, 2018, https://www.alphabeta.com/wp-content/uploads/2019/01/google-skills-report.pdf.

[6] McCrindle, The Future of Education, 2019, https://educationfuture.com.au/#eff-report.

[7] Daniel Goleman, *Emotional Intelligence: Why it can matter more than IQ*, Bantam, 2006.

[8] Brené Brown, *Daring Greatly: How the courage to be vulnerable transforms the way we live, love, parent and lead*, Avery, 2012.

[9] Daniel Flynn, *Chapter One*, The Messenger Group, 2016.

[10] Brené Brown, *The Gifts of Imperfection: Let go of who you think you're supposed to be and embrace who you are*, Simon & Schuster, 2010.

Chapter 8: Why work wellbeing is non-negotiable

[1] Australian Bureau of Statistics, Census of Population and Housing: Nature and Content, Australia 2016, Australian Government, Canberra, 2016, www.abs.gov.au.

[2] McCrindle, Work-Life Balance in Australia, 2017, https://mccrindle.com.au/insights/blogarchive/worklife-balance-in-australia/.

[3] Australian Bureau of Statistics, General Social Survey: Summary Results, Australia, 2014, 29 June 2015, https://www.abs.gov.au/ausstats/abs@.nsf/mf/4159.0.

[4] Reventure, A Future that Works, Workplace Wellbeing, 2017, http://www.afuturethatworks.org.au/reports.

[5] Australian Bureau of Statistics, Labour Force, Australia, June 2019, cat. 6202.0, https://www.abs.gov.au/ausstats/abs@.nsf/mf/6202.0.

[6] Triple J, What's Up in Your World, 2018, https://www.abc.net.au/triplej/programs/hack/whats-up-in-your-world-the-census-for-young-people/10051266.

[7] Australian HR Institute, Turnover and Retention Research Report, 2018, https://www.ahri.com.au/media/1222/turnover-and-retention-report_final.pdf.

[8] Arianna Huffington, *Thrive*, Harmony, 2014.

[9] Daniel Flynn, *Chapter One*, The Messenger Group, 2016.

Chapter 9: How to be a work wellbeing champion

[1] Daniel Goleman, *Emotional Intelligence*, Bantam, 2006.

[2] Arthur Asa Berger, The Meanings of Culture, http://journal.media-culture.org.au/0005/meaning.php.

[3] Brené Brown, *Daring Greatly: How the courage to be vulnerable transforms the way we live, love, parent and lead*, Avery, 2012.

[4] Ken Robinson, *Out of Our Minds: Learning to be creative*, John Wiley and Sons, 2001.

[5] Deloitte, The 2017 Deloitte Millennials Survey, Apprehensive millennials: seeking stability and opportunities in an uncertain world, 2017, bit.ly/ 2B1eVml.

[6] ibid.

[7] Reventure, A Future that Works, 2016 Snapshot of the Australian Workplace, 2016, http://www.afuturethatworks.org.au/reports.

[8] ibid.

[9] Stephen Covey, *The 7 Habits of Highly Effective People: Powerful lessons in personal change*, Free Press, 2004.

[10] Oxford Leadership, Collaborative Leadership White Paper, 27 August 2016, https://www.oxfordleadership.com/wp-content/uploads/2017/07/OL-White-Paper-Collaborative-Leadership.pdf.

[11] Patrick Lencioni, *The Five Dysfunctions of a Team*, Jossey-Bass, 2002.

[12] World Economic Forum, The Future of Jobs: Employment, Skills and Workforce Strategy for the Fourth Industrial Revolution, January 2016, http://www3.weforum.org/docs/WEF_Future_of_Jobs.pdf.

[13] AlphaBeta for Google Australia, Future Skills: The rise of machines will drive a need for more lifelong learning in Australia, 2018, https://www.alphabeta.com/wp-content/uploads/2019/01/google-skills-report.pdf.

Overview of research methodologies

[1] Work Wellbeing, www.workwellbeing.com.au.

[2] McCrindle, The Future of Education, 2019, https://educationfuture.com.au/#eff-report.

[3] Education Future Forum 2019, www.educationfuture.com.au.

[4] City Infield, Maximum Impact in Your Community, 2019, https://cityinfield.com/.

[5] Reventure, A Future that Works, 2016 Snapshot of the Australian Workplace, 2016, www.afuturethatworks.org.au.

[6] ibid.

[7] ibid.

INDEX